The I

*Memoir of a Young Boy
Growing Up in the Valley Town*

Allan Duffin

Copyright © 2023 *Allan Duffin*

All Rights Reserved

ISBN Paperback : 978-1-962893-70-1

Dedication

To My Daughter Kelly Duffin, for her unwavering faith in me that I could successfully complete a Book full of Boyhood Stories one day.

Acknowledgment

For Jean Zuliniak Quigley, Colleen Garry-Woods and the members of the Facebook Group, "If you grew up in Dundas" for their enthusiastic support in the creation of this Book.

Contents

Dedication i

Acknowledgment ii

About the Author vi

Foreward vii

Preface viii

Everyday Should Be Mother's Day: *A Son's Reflections* x

Chapter One A New Life in Dundas 1

Chapter Two The Melville Street Boarding House 10

Chapter Three Rummage Sales and Dinner Feasts 20

Chapter Four The Den of Iniquity and The Dentist 26

Chapter Five School Days and the Ugly Plaid Coat 31

Chapter Six The Homestead 40

Chapter Seven Pranks Aplenty 45

Chapter Eight Hide, Seek & Snacks 52

Chapter Nine Legendary Explorations 55

Chapter Ten The Dump 64

Chapter Eleven The Sailor 66

Chapter Twelve The Funeral Home 71

Chapter Thirteen Old Dundas Stores 75

Chapter Fourteen School Days 82

Chapter Fifteen Old Time Deliveries 91

Chapter Sixteen The Bus 96

Chapter Seventeen The Dances 103

Chapter Eighteen The Show	108
Chapter Nineteen Fun and Games	113
Chapter Twenty BAD BOYS	118
Chapter Twenty-One Working Boys	123
Chapter Twenty-Two Dog Days of Summer	129
Chapter Twenty-Three Suckers	136
Chapter Twenty-Four Rollers Skates and more Pranks	138
Chapter Twenty-Five Childhood Adventures	141
Chapter Twenty-Six Under Cover in the Dark	146
Chapter Twenty-Seven Gunpowder and Cannons	149
Chapter Twenty-Eight Soldiers	152
Chapter Twenty-Nine Dundas Entertainment	162
Chapter Thirty Winter Fun	171
Chapter Thirty-One The Telephone	175
Chapter Thirty-Two Halloween Haunts	180
Chapter Thirty-Three A Real Ghost	185
Chapter Thirty-Four Winter Adventures	191
Chapter Thirty-Five Historic Fires	194
Chapter Thirty-Six The Santa Suit and Other Christmas Stories	198
Chapter Thirty-Seven Some More Memories	205
Chapter Thirty-Eight Some Penneys for your Thoughts	213
Epilogue	217

About the Author

Allan Duffin was born in Hamilton, Ontario and his family moved to nearby Dundas in 1950 when his Father joined the Dundas Police Force. He was raised in Dundas spending over 20 years there. He went on to a career in EMS for over 40 years. He started as an Ambulance Medic in Burlington. Within a few years, he and a partner started the Halton-Mississauga Ambulance Service operating Ambulance Service in those regions.

He was the operations lead for the evacuation of the Mississauga Hospital and nearby Long Term Care Facilities during the Mississauga Train Chlorine Gas Derailment Emergency in November of 1979. The City's evacuation was the largest without loss of life or injury in the history of North America. In May of 1980, he again directed Operations for the evacuation of St. Joseph's Hospital in Hamilton, Ontario after an HVAC fire.

He left the Ambulance Service in 1985 accepting a position with Emergency Health Services, Ministry of Health and Long Term Care to manage the Mississauga Central Ambulance Communications Centre. In 1997 he returned to Hamilton to manage the Ambulance Communications Centre there. In 2001, he was promoted to the position of Regional Field Manager for Southwestern Ontario.

In September of 2008, he was presented with the EMS Exemplary Service Medal by Major General Richard Rohmer representing the Governor General of Canada. He retired in 2010.

His previous writing credits were for EMS-related magazines including Canadian Paramedicine. This personal memoir of his childhood is his first book.

Foreword

I first met Allan Duffin over 60 years ago when we both attended St. Augustines School in Dundas. I recall he was quite a character then, so it was no surprise to read about the various antics outlined in this book. I too went to a number of haunts herein described though our paths never crossed. His stories of his youth are amusing, sad, and some downright frightening. They take my back to my own childhood when it was a simpler uncomplicated life with many memories I had long forgotten.

Anyone growing up in Dundas in that era will remember many names and places from their own youth in many stories in this book and perhaps some local history unknown to many. In fact, anyone raised up in a Small Town anywhere will likely relate to their own names and places in many chapters of this book.

As I read these stories, I am reminded of the saying, "Boys will be Boys" which fits this Author's experiences to a tee. Sit back, turn the pages and enjoy like I did, reading of the escapades of a boy growing up in our Valley Town.

- *Jean Katherine Zuliniak-Quigley*

Preface

As titled, this book is a Memoir of a Young Boy who grew up in a small town in that truly nostalgic age of the 50's and 60's and most importantly, was raised by a Single Parent. Accordingly, the Book is dedicated to all Single Parents everywhere who sacrifice so much with their absolute dedication to raising their children.

Minnie Marguerite Duffin graced this earth from September 21, 1911 thru August 4, 1989. It is to this Woman, my Mother, who instilled so many values in me that I owe my later successes in life to. Widowed at 41 years of age with Three Children, my Mother continued a life of extreme challenges that began far back in her childhood. Being the eldest of 6 children, the heavy weight of responsibility enveloped her from an early age. Her Father, Sherman Huff was an unemployed Carpenter when he signed on with the Great Canadian Expeditionary Force in World War 1 as the pay commenced immediately. She was but 5 years old when he left for overseas.

Her Mother, Jessie Arnold Huff, managed to scrape by with the monthly income which for a Canadian Soldier at entry level was about $1.10 per day, less than that of a routine laborer in Canada at the time. My Mother's childhood was one of hardship such as being sent out with her younger sister to walk the Railway Tracks near their central Hamilton Home to collect coal that had fallen from Trains.

This was desperately needed to heat the home and provide cooking fuel for meals. Occasionally if a Train came by and the girls were noticed, the railway men would throw a few shovelfuls off for them to gather. Then as their fingers turned numb from the cold, they would head back home with their buckets amply filled. As she turned 17 in 1929, the Great Depression commenced a mere number of weeks later and as history records was fraught with hard times.

In 1935, she married William Duffin, my father who would go on to join the Hamilton Police Service and serve from 1941 thru 1949. They came to Dundas next though early in 1952, came my Father's untimely death at 39 years of age. Though he was a Police Officer, the municipal police wages were not significant and benefits if any were very meager until the Province of Ontario took over police responsibilities in the 1960's.

Though this book recounts a number of humorous family and personal memories it also illuminates my Mother's adaptability in managing to successfully raise our family by herself. Single Parent statistics of the early 1950's reflect a volume of only 9%. For my Mother, the fact she could not work beyond our home made her struggle even more so though it was blissfully unapparent to us children who never really went without.

While she appears in numerous scenarios described as overly strict and authoritative, it wasn't without love and after all, she had to be.

Allan and Mother Circa 1969.

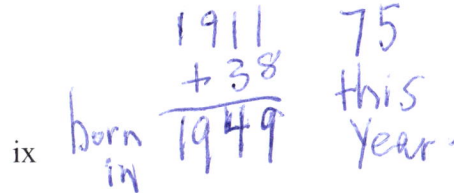

Everyday Should Be Mother's Day:
A Son's Reflections

Mother's Day is celebrated on the second Sunday in May. In Dundas there will be 1000's of Flowers delivered and many celebratory Dinners conducted. Some lucky Folks still have their Mothers many decades later in their lives.

There will be many of us who no longer have our Mother at least in the present sense and we all know others for whom this particularly Mother's Day will be extremely poignant given it might be the first to be experienced without them.

The definition of poignant is something that has a strong effect on emotions or the senses, especially smell. Many of us will identify with that. I have never forgotten the smell of my Mother's perfume and since she passed, I have never ever smelled it again. Though I couldn't tell you it's brand or name, I can mentally bring that scent back instantly at least in my mind. I also can recall a line or two of a lullaby she used to sing to me to sleep with.

I, of course, am providing a male point of view on Mothers which is for most, a soft affectionate secure sense versus the authoritarian side of the Father which the Mother could activate when required. In the old days, the phrase "Wait till your Father gets home" was a popular and oft-heard expression. In my case, my Mother adeptly played both roles as required given my Father's early passing. I certainly did get my well-deserved "spankings" too with whatever was at hand, belt, Ironing Cord, Wooden Spoon etc.

For those of us whose Mothers have passed there are distinct memories of them which are easily recalled. My Mother suddenly with 3 Fatherless children never got to visit a Restaurant. I recall when I became a young man I wanted to take her to a Fancy Restaurant on Mother's Day. In this area, it was the Plainsman Restaurant just outside of Town that was extremely popular on all Holidays. So I'd make a reservation and it would be an absolute Zoo when we arrived, crammed full of numerous Families experiencing their once fabulous Smorgasbord.

The Plainsman Restaurant

Waitresses took your drink order and cleared the plates while you lined up and heaped your plate with most foods you could imagine. We must have had dinner there for at least 25-30 years or more. More often than not our Waitress was a Mrs. Ferris who must have worked there forever. My Mother was so disappointed as she expected (and more than deserved) to be served directly with her meal. She wasn't impressed having to go and get it herself nor the abundance of somewhat exotic fare like Eel and Octopus!

Later in my life, I would drive over to Melville Street to pick her up for an outing. She would get into the Car and settle but as I went to drive away she would stop me. Out of the Car and back into the House she'd go to check the Ashtrays and/or make sure she'd unplugged the Iron etc. On other days after getting in the Car, she would momentarily settle, then immediately get our and stand on the sidewalk berating me for my strong garlicky breath and calling me names which would be non-politically correct to repeat today!

As many of my vintage will recall it was a different time and those considered foreigners in that era were not always viewed positively which was very unfair. Another of my Mother's traits was to loudly announce whatever was on her mind regardless of what that might be or who might be within earshot, often much to our embarrassment!

She was also well equipped with that 3rd eye behind her head and a good sense of sniffing out a lie, though I did manage to occasionally slip a few past her. She was, though, a Woman who did everything and never asked for help with a defiant pride!! When I think of her remembering her appearance it is always wearing an apron.

Maybe it was an accident as they say but I don't believe my birth was a planned event. My Mother was 38 years old with two children when I was born. My Sister recalled a neighbor asking her if we had company after spying on a baby carriage outside the House and was shocked to learn of my Mother's pregnancy which obviously had not been widely shared.

When she passed away on August 4, 1989, three months shy of my 40th Birthday, I was in Virginia Beach and my Sister somehow tracked me down. With a 9 year old Son and a 3 year old Daughter in tow we immediately left, returning home in time for the funeral. For me it was an exceedingly sad and long drive back with a never-ending video-like repeat of my life with her. As well there were endless questions and explanations of how and why the Angels had spirited Grandma away.

It was a very emotionally distraught visit to the Cattel and Eaton Funeral Home for me and as I leaned over to kiss her forehead, I was struck at how attractive she looked, no more lines of worry or tension after all those years. Later it came to me that it was her dentures which she very seldom wore saying they never fit right that had also aided in restoring her looks.

These are but a slight few of many, many memories of my Mother. I hope I have perhaps ignited a number for you of your Mother and though there is the official celebratory date each year, shouldn't everyday be Mother's Day?

Chapter One

A New Life in Dundas

The former Town of Dundas, Ontario, now part of the City of Hamilton and it's historic jewel, lays nestled beneath the ridges of the Niagara Escarpment at the western end of Lake Ontario. In 1949, my Father, William Duffin, joined the Police Department there. He had previously served with the Hamilton Police Service from 1941 thru 1949. He was well known in the area for his athletic prowess with the Hamilton Police Athletic Teams.

He was also highly regarded as a Coach in Youth Programs and took the Hamilton Tigers to the District Junior Lacrosse Championship in 1944. In 1946, he coached Hamilton's Mahoney Bears Football Team to the Hamilton Regional Football League Championship.

In early 1950 with his young family in tow, the move was made to Dundas, and he became it's Police Officer, Badge # 41.

Our initial residence was in the original Historic George Pirie House, which was located at 11 Foundry Street behind the famed Music Hall and is no longer there. Our Family was comprised of my Father, Mother, Minnie, Sister Carole Ann, then 14, and her younger Brothers, Billy, 7 and the one year older Toddler, yours truly.

King Street Dundas early 1960's

Continuing with his involvement with area sports, my Father became a member of the newly created Dundas Police Minor Hockey Executive. This group was formed to create Minor Hockey in Dundas and was comprised of the President, Police Chief Earl Jack, Constable Sam Eyre, Vice President, James Wadge Treasurer and my Father William (Bill) Duffin as Secretary. The Dundas (Grightmire) Arena was officially opened on December 14, 1950, with Canadian Skating sensation Barbara Ann Scott participating in the ribbon cutting. My Father was assigned to accompany her during her time in Dundas.

Barbara Ann Scott with Constable William Duffin

Dundas Area Construction Photo Dundas Museum and Archives

Unfortunately, the following year my Father took ill for an extended time period and although he briefly returned to his Dundas Police Officer duties, he passed away at only 39 in early February of 1952.

The Funeral Service was conducted at St. Augustine's Church on Sydenham Street and was attended by a large contingent of Police Officers from Dundas, Hamilton and the Ontario Provincial Police lining both sides of Melville Street from Cross Street over to Sydenham Road. The Knights of Columbus provided an Honour Guard with their ceremonial swords drawn at the Church front, and the Funeral Procession to the Holy Sepulcher Cemetery in Burlington was over 2 miles long.

In truth, at only 26 months old, I have little recollection of my Father and provide these details as told to me by my Mother and Siblings and also from Family Scrapbooks and the History of Dundas itself. A Tribute was paid to my Father for his efforts on behalf of the youth of Dundas at a benefit night a few weeks after his Death. An excerpt from the book "Dundas 1947-1973" by L. Button follows. On February 26th, over 2,500 people turned out to a Benefit sponsored by the Hamilton and Dundas Police Associations at the Dundas Arena. A Game was staged between the Hamilton/Dundas and City of Windsor Police Hockcy Teams. Mayor John Don expressed the sentiments of all gathered there that evening. "We all know the great work with youth that Bill Duffin was noted for, and this large gathering tonight is a tribute to the memory of the man, who during his short span of life, offered so much time and energy to young men". . ."

At that time, the Salary, Wage and benefits for Police Officers were not at today's levels, and my Mother, now a Widow with 3 Children, would be faced with a financial hardship. The funds raised at this event, plus a Women of the Moose Benefit Evening, were provided to my Mother. This allowed for a down payment for a House at 44 Melville Street destined to become the Duffin Homestead. That House was purchased for the tidy sum of $8,000 dollars. For my Mother, however, now a Widow with 3 Children, employment was out of the question, and some social assistance, then known as "Mothers Allowance," and other innovative measures would be required to support our Family.

The House built and still standing today on the Sydenham Street slope featured a completely self-contained lower section with a private entrance off Sydenham Street.

Former Duffin Homestead on Melville Street today

Rented out, those Tenants provided significant support towards the costs of maintaining our Home. It was a 3 3-bedroom house and would be quite full for a number of years. Those Bedrooms upstairs were rented out initially to my Uncle Tommy and Aunt Gladys Heugh and their young Daughter, my Cousin Lois. To help with her limited income, my Mother also took on the laundry requirements of the St. Augustine's Priests, including the washing and pressing of the Church Linens.

Interesting to note that the house next door at the corner of Sydenham in the summer of 2023 was listed for over a million dollars. Check out the listing and price for our old house beside it in 1979 before the Neighborhood became the fashionable Heritage District. Had we only known the shapes of things to come?

44 MELVILLE ST(4-1)$46,900(CASH)   Z13926D

As I look back now, as a Toddler, those circumstances were, for the most part, beyond my knowledge and comprehension. For my Brother and Sister, though, it was a significant change, and my Sister was devastated as a teenager at the loss of her Father, who being his Daughter of course, was very close to him. She talked of him often, with me sharing many stories. One day which I will never forget, she took me to the Arena, showing me the "Bill Duffin Memorial Trophy," which had been created for Minor Hockey to award "Good Sportsmanship." There I was, this small boy straining on my tip toes to get a look at it high up in the Trophy Case on the Lobby wall. Sadly, many years later, upon inquiring about its whereabouts, we learned that it had been placed in storage during some renovations and had been destroyed by water damage. We have no photo of that trophy.

As Children during that time, we never realized it, but my Mother's social activity, considering my Father's numerous social circles and sporting events, came to an abrupt end. With her strong will and determination, though, she carried on and seldom complained about her fate as a Single Parent. As for us Kids, we journeyed onward happy and as comfortable as we could be. Yes, there were occasional wardrobe supplements from church sales, but we always started the 1st day of School in new clothes. For me, though, it never seemed to take long to acquire the stains or tears in them.

I wonder how many former Boys out there would remember the "Iron On Patches" that covered the holes and well well-worn spots in the knees and Butts part of your pants. They became a necessary part of my wardrobe. I recall a knock at the Door one Christmas, and there stood Mr. Fiorvanti, the Owner of the IGA Store at Miller's Lane and King Street, with a Turkey and bags of groceries. I recall sensing my Mother's embarrassment while she graciously declined requesting that these groceries be sent to another Household where they might be desperately needed. Someone with good intentions had obviously nominated our family. Food was never an issue, though, and we never went without a Turkey on any of the major holidays.

Meanwhile, the occupation of the upper floors of the House continued. My Aunt and Uncle moved out within a year or so, finding a lower-level apartment next door, and were replaced by a couple fresh off the Boat from London, England. They did not stay long as the Missus became homesick and sailed back to England with her Husband soon following.

Next came the Beli Family, who had journeyed to Dundas from Italy. With limited English skills, communication at times with my Mother was challenging, but they managed. My Mother's basic spices for cooking then were Salt, Pepper and Sage for the Turkey Dressing. While Mrs. Beli's English may have been challenged, her cooking skills were formidable, and she managed to create fabulous culinary concoctions like Ravioli from scratch with just a hot plate upstairs and occasionally sharing our Oven. Strong and delicious smells of food often filled the House from her magically created sauces, and then much to my Mother's dismay, I discovered and learned to love Garlic!

The Beli's had a Son named Tino, my Brother's age, and they became fast friends. Tino attended St. Augustine's School with my Brother, often staying after class for English lessons. A year later, he was fully conversational, being proficient too, even with the bad words we weren't supposed to say! From what my Brother recalls, he may have also set a record too for the number of times he got the strap at school. The Beli Family stayed for a few years, then eventually vacated our upstairs for their new Homeland, Ohio in the USA and once again, change would happen in our Home.

Chapter Two

The Melville Street Boarding House

David Hood was a longtime friend of our Family and had lived alone in a Room in the Melbourne Hotel. Learning of our vacancy, he then moved into an upstairs room and became our First "Boarder," paying for his room, laundry service and meals. He worked as a Supervisor in the "Breakers Testing" section of Westinghouse on Longwood road in Hamilton. Breakers are basically your off-and-on wall switches, and I suspect there are thousands of that product he oversaw still in use today in this area.

Dave was a lifelong Dundas Resident who once delivered groceries by Horse and Wagon for Powell's' Grocery Store, whose original location now houses the Thirsty Cactus, a popular Road House.

About 1907: Entry in Civic Holiday Parade - H. F. Powell, Grocer.

He had a Car!!! Now, I got to go on great adventures with him, like into the Beverly Swamp, where we would stop and wash the Car with the roadside water. Our House, circa 1840's, had no external tap fixture or hose.

As the Family continued to evolve, more changes came, my Sister left for an early marriage then my Brother's enlistment to the Royal Canadian Navy left me as an only child. I actually loved it, finally getting my own Bedroom!

At some point thereafter, we also had my then-single Uncle Gord come and board with us as well. Dave was our early riser and was always the first up to put the coffee on. My Mother would get up a bit later and make everyone's lunch before waking us, kids. Dave would sit in our Rocking Chair in the kitchen beside Toby, our Blue Budgie. Toby had great character, and he'd listen attentively when you spoke to him. When he decided to speak, it was crystal clear. Dave would literally talk his ear off, repeating various phrases over and over on those early mornings.

My Mother had 3 Sisters and 2 Brothers and would occasionally host Special Holiday Dinners. With a festive gathering of Diners in our large kitchen, the Bird would get excited! Dinner would just be served, and then Toby would let loose with a volley of rude and uncomplimentary remarks about a number of people around the table, including my Grandmother. My Mother, horrified, would scold the Bird and give Dave "the look" while we Kids were in hysterics. A few years later, at Breakfast one morning, Toby just fell over and died. We soon acquired another Budgie, green this time whose name escapes me now, but he just sat there like a Tree Trunk and never spoke.

Now operating a full-fledged "Boarding House," my Mother provided 5 5-star services, and when it came to food, she made sure no one could ever leave the table hungry. The problem for us was we weren't all "grown-up hard-working men!" The lunches, though, came off the assembly line accordingly and, to our friends at School, were legendary. Two sandwiches, a Bologna with Mustard plus Peanut Butter and Jam, along with a half-pound wedge of cake with creamy icing! My Brother Billy used to barter his lunch items for cigarettes though he'd tell my Mother how much he enjoyed his lunch.

We learned it wasn't a good idea to bring any lunch home. Good thing today's custom of sending home uneaten lunches from school wasn't a practice back then. Dinner, though, was a whole different experience! The only dishes on the table were our plates and silverware. My Mother, with various Pots in hand, would circle around the table, piling up the meat and potato potato-like fare on your plate. We, "non Hungry, not Working Men," were expected to feast accordingly and could not leave the table until our plates were empty.

Dave would drive Mother to an Apple Orchard someplace in Ancaster where she would buy cheaper bruised "Windfall Apples" for pies and puddings. So the table literally groaned under the weight of dinner. I didn't even have a Dog to sneak any to! Now Lima Beans, to this day, are on my avoid at all costs list. Just imagine their fabulous texture ice cold an hour after dinner, as I sat imprisoned at the table, like biting down on a Beetle! It was a battle of wills which I always lost except the day when I hurled them up on a Halloween, itching to get out there!

My Friends, after participating once in our unique Dinning Experience, always politely declined all future Dinner Invitations. It was exciting, though, when I got invited elsewhere and learned of the "Pass the Peas Please" concept, where dinner was set in large bowls on the table, and you could take only what you wanted to eat at the time. So yes, we never ever were hungry, but growing up that way, my not exactly thin waistline today is a testament to my life long struggle with portion sizes.

Growing up in a small town like Dundas, at least back in the 50's and 60's, from my recollection, was very relaxed as opposed to the nearby bustling City. It was a gentler time period where many Folks left their doors unlocked and, of course, their Children with considerably more freedom than today.

Originally the youngest of 3 Children, with a 6-7-year gap between each, I found myself as noted, alone with the House to myself. In the absence of my Sister and Brother though, came new responsibilities and adventures. While my shopping expeditions on my own had been limited to an occasional visit to a Variety Store like Oneil's or Wilson's for candy, anywhere else was always with my Mother.

My first singular adventure was being sent to Kelday's Tobacco Store, which was located on the southeast side of King Street at Memorial Square. With my note firmly clenched in my hand, I walked into the store and nervously stood there while Mr. Kelday peered over his glasses at me, saying, "what can I do for you?" Trembling, I placed my scrunched-up note on the Counter, and he picked it up, unfolded it and placed a package of Export Plain end cigarettes on the counter. "36 Cents, please". I slid my similar scrunched scrunched-up Dollar Bill towards him, and he smiled, returning my change, and advised, "Now you take these cigarettes right back home to your Mother now".

Keldays Tobacco Store

Dundas Museum and Archives

Accordingly, proud of my accomplishment, I marched back up Sydenham Street and home.

Today, of course, with stricter laws, that couldn't happen. The next time it was to Newitt's, the Butcher, with another note. After sliding a few times on the saw saw-dusted floor, Mr. Newitt sternly reminded me what I was there for with a "are you buying something?" My Mother never let me slide in there either. Once again, I placed my note on the counter, and within a few minutes came the announcement, "2 lbs of Ground Chuck, 86 cents, please".

Newitts Butcher Shop

Dundas Museum and Archives

Now this time, no one suggested I go right Home and having run into some friends along the way, I was a bit waylaid. While I don't recall that distraction in detail now, I certainly do remember arriving home later without the meat! As it was unable to be found, the second order at 93 cents was funded from my allowance!

Funny, today it's regular, medium, lean and extra lean, no longer ground chuck, which I think was medium. It's also interesting these days that in many of the Grocery Stores, I swear it's only the label title and price that are different. The extra lean and medium sometimes all look the same, and I buy the medium in those circumstances.

A later assignment I recall was being sent to buy some Turnips, and being older, I refused a note stating I didn't require one as I could clearly read. I returned home, having failed at my mission and explaining there weren't any. I don't recall what grocery store it was, but my Mother later discovered there was certainly no shortage of Turnips. But I had no idea that they were also known and labelled as Rutabagas, which looked like a foreign language to me!

A few other memorable shopping stories that come to mind are with Drug Stores. My Sister once told me that in her early Teens, when having to purchase sanitary pads, she had to check to see if Clare Crozier, who lived a few doors down the Street from us, was working at Ralph's Drug Store. If he was, it would be too embarrassing, and she would have to go down to the IDA Drug Store and buy them there instead.

For me, it was my first ever purchase of, um, well, Condoms, and I sure as hell wasn't buying them in Dundas!! So here I was in the sprawling Metropolis of the little Town of Cayuga near Lake Erie in a Drug Store, wandering about until the last Woman had left. Then under the scrutiny of an Elderly Druggist, he peered over his glasses at me as well! Of course, as we older Folks know, back then, they were sold behind the counter and had to be asked for.

Do you have any idea how difficult it is to say Prophylactic while stammering? "Hi, I'd like to buy some, er Propa lic tack, er proba teak um um. With no smile and a quavering squeaky voice, he barked out, "Are you asking for condoms, boy?" Now burning red and feeling like I have shrunk two feet, I stammer out yes expecting to be thrown out of the store but instead he reached under the counter and sold them to me. It was the quickest exit from a store I'd ever make.

When we decided to go fishing in the Marsh (Cootes Paradise), Norman's Mother would make us Cornmeal Balls, which we would use for bait to catch Carp. One time on a Saturday, we sold a 5-6 lb Carp for 5 bucks to a Man who was walking thru the Marsh in a fancy suit after attending a Religious Service in nearby Westdale.

For our regular bait, we often went Worm Picking on area lawns, and I remember being chased off the chiropractor's Lawn at Park and Sydenham Streets. Some people didn't like worms being picked from their lawns. We christened him the Worm Hog!

I wonder if anyone of that era remembers the elderly Lady who walked the streets dressed in black wearing spectacles and a black Pill Box Hat with a matching veil over her face. One night we got this great idea to pick worms in the Grove Cemetery thinking those occupants wouldn't be complaining. It was dark, of course, and we had our headband flashlights. Hearing a noise, we looked up, and there was the old lady dressed in black. I think the can of worms must have gone 20 feet up in the air as we ran for our lives!!

At a younger age, I recall being at Gerry Aussem's House, which was 4 doors up York Road from the Cemetery Gates. Living on Melville Street, it was much shorter to walk home thru the Cemetery and Dundas Driving Park than go the long way around down to Park St and across.

One night in the winter, I stayed there later in the afternoon, and it had got dark. I had mentioned my nervousness about walking thru the Cemetery in the dark though If I went a long way around, I would be late for Dinner. With his older brother Peter, we went down stairs to his Dad's workshop and took a baby food jar, filled it with some finishing nails and boiled hot water in a kettle and put the jar in a bag. I took it with me, ready to swing it at anything that might jump out at me in the Cemetery. Fortunately, I didn't encounter anyone, but it was terrifying walking thru there in the dark.

As many of you older Folks would know, back in the day, there were a number of Fire Alarm boxes located throughout many communities, including Dundas. It was a Red Box with a white door handle fastened to a telephone pole. While I remember a number of them, one I specifically remember was on Cross Street at the eastern end of Melville Street, a block from my house.

While I certainly cannot recite the history of these boxes, presumably, they were created at a time when many homes did not have telephones. A Fire Alarm would activate a loud Fog Horn like wail from the Dundas Fire Department Tower in Memorial Square.

Anyone who ever heard that unique sound, like a ship lost in the fog, could never forget it. Volunteers hearing it's echoing wail would accordingly travel quickly to the Fire Hall, and acquiring the Box location would respond in Fire Trucks.

As a Kid, I was always fascinated by these boxes. Another of my many boyhood friends was Connel Hansen, who I kicked around with in the mid-sixties. A local urban legend was that if you pulled one of those alarms, your hand would be bathed in a red dye. One Saturday, while walking down from the Park, we came upon that box and stood there discussing this.

So there we were, looking at this box, and Connel suddenly jumped up, pulling the handle down, having pulled the sleeve of his coat up over his hand to catch any dye that might spill out. Once you pulled the box door open, there was a lever that you had to pull down. He pulled it down, and the Hooter, as we used to call it, started its mournful wail but no red dye!

There were a number of younger neighborhood kids watching this. We took off back to my house, where no one was home. I busted my Piggy Bank, and we managed to catch the Roxy Theatre Matinee being out of sight.

I remember sitting there in the Theatre, gloating at our success. At the end of the Show, we parted, Connel lived up in Flamboro near the Circle M Ranch. I walked up Sydenham Street to Melville and froze seeing a Police Car in front of the House! The Neighborhood Children had been only too happy to rat us out!

I was grounded for an eternity once more. My Mother certainly had her trials and tribulations with my upbringing!

Chapter Three

Rummage Sales and Dinner Feasts

One of the interesting things I recall about growing up long ago in Dundas was its number of Churches in close proximity to each other in what is now called the Heritage District". From our House on Melville near Sydenham, there were 4 different Churches within one and a half blocks. St. Augustine's Roman Catholic on Sydenham, St. James Anglican just up Melville Street, the Knox Presbyterian just down Melville Street and St. Paul's United a block down at Park and Cross Streets.

Despite our different religious affiliations, most kids played together in our day to -to-day adventures, and many of our Mothers knew each other well. I learned that on shopping excursions with my Mother, asking "who was that lady?" Questions when she'd stop to chat. In today's vernacular, that meant "shared intelligence," which resulted in little white lie discoveries on occasion. As for the Churches, I got to visit all of them as a small boy with my Mother. We'd go to their Rummage Sales!

While Yard Sales in this day and age are common, back in the day, it was the Churches that had the monopoly. My Mother never missed one, and I always considered it a great adventure. We'd arrive there early, about 15 minutes before the Doors opened. I never forgot the first one, mostly ladies lining up. Some rather stout ones with "Popeye" like arms would charge thru the line as the doors opened.

Petrified, I held on to a knotted clump of my Mother's Skirt as this value value-crazed mob closed together, thundering into the Church Hall. Had I tripped, I am sure I would have been trampled to an early end. As I think back now, it seemed that anyone displaying the slightest timidity would be shoved aside as they grappled for the

Bargains. My Mother, who my Father had christened "Dynamite," was all of 5' 2" but never gave an inch!

She would come away gloating over the fancy Tea and Saucer Cups she'd bought, 10 or 25 cents each. I remember asking why she didn't buy the whole set which of course there wasn't. They went into a small glass door cabinet in the Living Room. For me I might acquire some gently used clothes, but more importantly, I always came away with a well-worn Toy too. All religious aspects aside, one time I brought an Ouija Board home too from a Church Sale! Many years later, when our House was sold in 1979, we held an Auction for several of its contents. My Mother sat there incredulous as some of those Tea and Saucer sets she'd paid small change for went for 25 to 50 dollars apiece.

While I was certainly raised quite healthy, with the nutrition of the day at the forefront, what I was made to eat was occasionally, was simply "gross" to me. As I experienced the smell, taste and texture of some food items, it was all I could do to get them down.

Most vegetables were served from the Can in our House, and though I enjoy peas today, they have to be fresh or frozen. For my taste buds, Peas or most other canned vegetables are the last thing you'll find on my table.

Housewives of my Mother's vintage were raised in the Depression, challenging times for being able to afford and acquire fresh food. There were no refrigerators back then, and even in my youth, it was an icebox in our Kitchen until I was at least 10 years old. So usually around once a week, the Iceman came by. Down our Hallway, he'd come with his Tongs gripping a sizeable block of Ice to be deposited in the top of our Icebox. You had to keep an eye on the water tray at the bottom, which needed to be emptied as the Ice Melted. One day around 1958, Dave Hood, who was now my quasi Step Father, came home with a Fridge!!

There had been an Employee Scratch and Dent sale at Westinghouse. It was a small single-door fridge that actually did have a dent in the top of the door, looking like someone had hit it with a Baseball Bat! But the door did still close and seal properly. There was lots of excitement as my Brother and Mother helped him carry it into the House. There wasn't much of a freezer at the top either, I mean, it wouldn't even keep Ice Cream properly, but it did have Ice Cube trays that froze, and I loved to make them.

At Christmas time, my Mother would put me to work making fancy ones. I would sit at the kitchen table with a jar of maraschino cherries, carefully plunking one in each cube slot and then covering them over with water. I was impressed and was actually even allowed to have a drink of pop with one in it, but only one. The balance was reserved for our Christmas Guests. That 1958 Fridge later made it's way to the Ambulance Service in Oakville and somehow lasted until the late 1980's.

Now let me tell you more about that Boarding House Food. In my childhood, I had to eat Turkey at least 3 times per year at Easter, Thanksgiving and Christmas, of course. Talk about gross, my Mother roasted it in our old Gas McClary Oven. No Pilot light either, you had to strike a match to light it. Given the earlier challenges of meat preservation that my Mother grew up with, she made sure any meat would be safe by cooking it extremely well done! After she finished with it, a Turkey Breast was akin to rawhide! Even the Dark Meat had a mummified appearance and texture! I won't even mention Liver!

It was simply a rite of passage growing up to chew these things and enjoy a few other choice delicacies, including Pickled Beets, Beans and Parsnips and of course, Lima Beans. I couldn't tell you now how she cooked Parsnips, but there was a strong smell all through the House of a Men's Locker Room, and unless there was a raging blizzard, I'd go outside. It was another toxic like veggie and was one thing I absolutely refused to allow past my lips though today I wouldn't make a stew without one!

Then, one day something rather miraculous happened. It was Christmas, and some Aunts, Uncles and Cousins were coming for Dinner. I'd be around 12 or so, and I was allowed to make alcoholic drinks. I would put two of those fancy ice cubes in a glass, then fill this special little glass to the marked line with various flavors of booze. Then I'd add the mix, and finally, with the handle of a teaspoon, stir it well, then deliver it to the guests, my Mother included.

It was a total Zoo in the House, with people everywhere. My Sister, of course, always helped put these Dinners together with my Mom. So on this particular day, she passes by me and whispers get your Mother another drink! So I go to get her glass, and I notice it is only half empty. I tell my Sister, who sternly insists to add another shot of liquor and refilling the glass! Being an obedient youngster, I do what I am told though wondering why!

Sister Carole Ann and Mother in Kitchen

A while later, my Sister was escorting my slightly now tipsy Mother to the Living Room to visit with the Guests telling her she would finish up in the kitchen. Sitting at the kitchen table mixing more drinks, I notice my Sister cranking the heat down in the Oven while promising me an ill fate should I say anything! At Dinner, it was the first time I had ever enjoyed Turkey being so moist and flavorful. I also recall my Mom wasn't feeling so great the next day either.

Along the edges of our backyard sidewalk was home to some rather slimy snails. They had little antennae-like feelers or whatever they were called, and I would keep them in a jar sometimes. Thank God Mom never cooked any of them then, but I thought I'd mention them here for Folks who gag at the thought of Escargot. Just so you know, it isn't those Dundas Snails, they actually come in a can from France and are delicious in garlic butter, really!

Tales of my Mother's cuisine wouldn't be complete without mentioning steak too. In our house, given its expense, it was a rare menu offering and about as appetizing as the leather from a shoe, cooked until petrified! So later, at 16 years old, there I was on a Dinner Date with a young lady, and we were at the Golden Steer Steakhouse on Dundurn Street in Hamilton, which I have had saved up for, forever. Along comes the Waitress, who asks the young lady how she would like her steak done, to which she replies, "Medium rare".

As you can appreciate by now, the Boarding House "Beaver" here has never been asked a question about what he'd like to eat. It had only been the statement, "Eat whatever I put in front of you or else!!" So wishing to impress, I reply, "I'll have mine medium rare too," with no idea, of course, of how it might taste. Well, I loved it, and you know that was the only Steak House I visited for a long time before I learned about how meat could be cooked the same way anywhere else.

Hamilton Spectator

Chapter Four

The Den of Iniquity and The Dentist

I had heard of the Den of Iniquity long before I actually experienced it. In fact, for a long while, I wasn't sure what an Iniquity was. My imagination conjured up a number of possibly frightening scenarios. I think I was likely around 3 years old when my Sister Carole Ann, who was 14 years my senior, took me there to the Deluxe Restaurant. All of us had been historically forbidden to ever set foot in the place. It was one of my Mother's mantras "The Deluxe Restaurant is a Den of Iniquity". To this day, I am not sure if even she had ever set foot in there.

Deluxe Restaurant Crush Foto

In retrospect, it was likely a theme heavily influenced by my then-late Father, the Police Officer. I suppose that from a Policeman's viewpoint, any place with Motorcycles parked in front was of questionable merit. With my Sister's advanced age came the responsibility of being stuck with me often. Accordingly, when she wanted to go someplace, I'd get dragged along. As a youngster, I couldn't manage Carole Ann and out would come "Can" which I would call her forever more.

My Mother, had she known, would have been horrified of me being introduced to that Den and it's cast of characters. While I will admit to nervously glancing around for Iniquities the first time there, that worry faded quickly when I was introduced to Cokes and bags of Chips! Albeit, I was made to solemnly swear that I would not mention where we'd been to my Mother. As for Iniquities, I never noticed any, and I discovered that it really was a cool place.

Photo M. Zuliniak

Photo M. Zuliniak

My Sister would squeeze me into a booth, and she'd sit there exchanging teenage gossip with her friends. I didn't care, I had my Pop and Chips and a magic box on the wall that made the music play throughout the Restaurant! I also got to watch the odd cockroach scurry across the top of the booth. Though not shown in this photo, in those early days of the Deluxe Restaurant, there was a large Aquarium behind the Soda Fountain Counter with huge Goldfish swimming about.

One of those motorcycles parked in front belonged to my Brother's friend Walter Rogerson. Walter, who they nicknamed "Tex," had huge boots and was a fixture there. He had me convinced he'd been a Cowboy once in Texas. He would be slouched down in a booth, his long legs and boots extended. When he stood, I'd be fixated by the huge Belt Buckle at eye level with me. He told great stories, too, like the time a rattle snake had curled up on his belly while he slept. As well he liked Johnny Cash, and I must have heard the song "Ring of Fire" from that Jukebox a 100 times over the years.

Later, I discovered one of my classmates was his little Sister Moira. The Deluxe Restaurant was owned and operated by Du and Sue Wong. Du garbed in his white Chef's attire, ran the kitchen while

Sue, clothed in a green waitress outfit with a black sweater coat, Kleenex in a pocket, waited on the tables and cashed the customers out. She certainly knew us Duffin Kids well, unknown to my Mother for a number of years. My Sister Carole actually worked there later as a waitress for some time. I loved to go there, especially on Hot Summer Days, reveling in my first experience with air conditioning!! I don't recall their Chinese Food, but I can still taste the excellent Burgers and Fries I ate there and my first introduction to lettuce, tomato and onion on a Burger!

I understand that it was Du who had the passion for owning a Restaurant, and when he passed away in the early 70's, Sue closed the Door but left it all intact. Who knew then that this place of once questionable reputation would go on to become a time capsule of its age, then later a famous film landmark graced by Robin Williams and many other Actors. For many years, the Deluxe Restaurant became synonymous with the Town of Dundas itself, and though now gone, the Bangkok Spoon Deluxe continues in its place as a Community favorite for Thai and other Asian-inspired food offerings. One Booth of the original Deluxe remains in history and is now an exhibit in the Dundas Museum.

At the somewhat tender age of 6-7, my Mother took me downtown on a Mystery Trip. Although I didn't realize it at the time, my older Brother Billy had told me about this scary place. Had I known in advance, she may not have got me out the door! In a roundabout way, we walked west from Memorial Square on the south side of King Street, a bit past Cowper's Hardware, and then stopped at a Doorway beside Morden's Bakery.

I remember when she opened the door, there was a long flight of stairs. For the first few steps, there was an incredible waft of delicious bakery smells, enough to make you drool! But a few more steps up, it was a vastly different strong oil of cloves-like smell. Gasping, I held my Nose as she pulled me up those stairs.

We continued on to the top, arriving at the office of a well-known Dundas Dentist, who my Brother had said was scary! To this day, the memories of that Dentist's Office for me are in Black and White. We had barely sat down in that waiting room when there was a loud commotion, and a Grown Man rushed out of a doorway, still wearing his stained dental bib, and he bounded down the stairs. I sat there paralyzed with fear. Momentarily later, an older scary, looking Nurse like woman stepped out of that very doorway and announced in a loud voice, "Allan Duffin, NEXT".

My Mother managed to grab me halfway down the stairs and literally drag me back. My memories of that Dentist were that he was old with jet-black hair and glasses that looked like Coke Bottle bottoms. Doctors are often described by their "Beside Manner". Perhaps for a Dentist, it would be "Mouth side Manner," but in any case, he had little patience with children. I don't recall being strapped in the chair, but he and his Nurse literally growled me into submission. As he drilled holes in my teeth with what seemed like an early Stonehenge-like tool, it made a horrible grinding noise and an awful burning smell. I am not sure he provided freezing all of the time either, as every now and then, he'd hit a nerve, and my legs would thrash out of the chair as if I had been given an electrical shock.

If you survived reasonably well, you were awarded with a rather primitive chalk Animal Figurine after being warned about the evils of candy. Not wanting to ever darken his doorway again, I brushed my teeth every day like a fiend, but it really didn't matter. A year later, I'd be back there enjoying another drilling!

As Radio Commentator Paul Harvey used to say, "Now here is the rest of the story". That Dentist, Dr. Arthur Hill, obviously knew what he was doing in the technical sense, and I have heard numerous compliments from a number of other Dentists over the years who have checked these now ancient fillings still in my teeth today. I also learned that Dr. Hill was a very well respected Dentist and was also the President of the Hamilton Area Dentist's Association for a number of years.

Chapter Five

School Days and the Ugly Plaid Coat

When I started School, I was fortunate to live exactly 2 blocks from St. Augustine's Elementary School. Though I have absolutely no memory of this, Duffin Family lore recounts the story of my first day there in Kindergarten. My Mother had escorted me in the morning, noting my curiosity outweighed any trepidation. Mid-morning attending to some gardening, she looked up to see me coming down Sydenham Street with my arm around the neck of a little blond girl. No one seems to recall who she was or if it was of mutual fondness or an outright kidnapping. In any case, my newfound friend and I were promptly marched back up the street to the school. I mean, hey, what did I know about recess? They let me out, and I found some company and left.

St. Augustine's School

Later, as a Grade 1 student, I had a Nun for my Teacher, Sister A. For you non-Catholics, all nuns are called sisters by their first name, and who could forget Whoopi Goldberg playing Sister Delores? I remember Sister A, though, as tall, thin and with thick glass spectacles. Anyway, one day, one of my classmates took an unscheduled dump which soon became evident from a familiar smell. I won't embarrass anyone here because I honestly do not remember who filled their pants. What I do recall, though, was that one by one, each classmate was called up to the front of the class and sniffed! Yes, sniffed. I don't know really otherwise how to describe it, but obviously, it left a considerable impression on me. I don't think my Mother believed me when I told her later what had happened.

At some point in my pre-teens (early 60's), an ugly plaid coat was provided for me. It was a bit longer than what I considered a normal coat to be and had a horrible green plaid design. It looked like something a young Girl in England might wear! I refused to wear it initially, and after a prolonged verbal tirade between my Mother and I, she relented, advising I could go to school without it if I wished.

Pleased at my victory, I set out for school; however, given it was January, I only made it about a block and, totally frozen, came back home and put it on. As anticipated, once I arrived at school, I was the laughing stock of my peers. Between the coat, though, and my red face, I have to admit I was warm.

A few weeks later, on the Spencer Creek, my friends and I happened upon a large metal gasoline can on its side stuck in the ice. Immediately, we took turns jumping on the can, trying to force it under the ice. This went on for quite a few minutes. Now at my next turn, it happened, swoosh, under the ice went the can along with the lower half of my body. Fortunately, with the help of my friends and my ugly plaid coat jamming up the hole, I did not go completely under the ice, and they managed to pull me out.

Walking home in water water-logged boots and clothes that were freezing was an unpleasant journey, to be sure, as was the anticipation of how I would be received upon arrival. Finding no one home, I was elated but now had to devise a plan quickly to dry my clothes.

Most homes then relied on Clotheslines for drying and, in January, reeled them in like frozen cardboard. Our House, circa 1840's, had no central heat. We had two Coal Burning Stoves. A large Quebec Heater in the Living room and a small flat top with two openings in the kitchen. Carefully, I laid my coat and pants across the kitchen stove and went upstairs to change my clothes.

Coming downstairs, the House reeked of a strong burning odor emanating from the kitchen, where my coat and clothes lay smoldering on the stove. Quickly grabbing them, I ran out the back door as I heard the front door opening. As I sat in the back shed pondering a number of excuses I might come up with, the shed door opened, and there she stood like a mini King Kong, arms folded and glowering at me!

The fact that it was, after all, an accident garnered me no sympathy whatsoever, and yep, I was incarcerated again for a few weeks, but at least I got a new coat that was not embarrassing.

Dundas Driving Park Entrance Dundas Museum and Archives

The Dundas Driving Park is a short two two-block distance down Alma Street from St. Augustine's School. In the 50's, there were Ponies stabled at the Park and at it's far end, there was a circular wooden ring where they gave Pony Rides on weekends. We often played in the Park at lunch hour. I won't mention names here, and I don't remember who decided to throw the first of what we called horse balls. They were though perfectly rounded and, when relatively fresh, splattered good when you hit your target. If you were involved in such skirmishes, you would surely recall that distinct odor!

Now after a rousing game, we were back in the class room. It didn't take long for one of the Girls to complain about the stench, whining they were about to throw up! Though no one admitted to anything, it didn't take Mrs. Denomme long (yep, more sniffing) to identify the culprits and home we were sent. Now not having far to walk, I quickly tried to come up with a reason why I am arriving early and smelly. My excuse for slipping and falling in the ring didn't carry any weight, especially since I had co-conspirators having the same issue. In the end, it was a wasted effort anyway, as the School had already called and provided sufficient evidence to get me grounded the following weekend.

Somewhere around grade 3 or so, when reading lessons happened, a group of 4 or 5 of us would be brought up to the front of the classroom. Positioned in a semi-circle, we would stand there and, at the direction of the Teacher, take turns reading a few paragraphs each. One afternoon after lunch during this session, I was totally engrossed in whatever we were reading. Mentally in a faraway land when the splattering sound brought me back to the Beans and Weiner Chunks flowing across the floor. One of our fellow readers must have had the flu. Though a few kids were gagging, we had to stay there while Primo, our Janitor, was summoned to clean it up, spreading the sawdust liberally.

Now in the later years at St. Augustine's, Mr. Troy came along. This was new and different in that all of my previous Teachers had been Nuns or Women. Mr. Troy was a no-nonsense Teacher, just what I needed, at least from my Mother's perspective. Smoking, as we know, was prevalent back then, and Mr. Troy actually gave us a "lesson one day about how Smoking was a danger to our health."

I don't know if the lesson was planned or if he suddenly had an urge for a smoke. Which of course, we didn't realize at the time. Out came a white handkerchief and then a cigarette which he lit. After a few puffs, he inhaled it thru the handkerchief and then showed us the nicotine stain on it, saying how it would mark our lungs that way. As most of our parents smoked at home, as did the Television Stars of the day, I don't think any of us kids thought much of it at the time.

One day while he was bent over a few desks ahead of me helping someone, I threw a Banana at David Penney. "Who did that?" Mr. Troy roared! There wasn't a sound, but with 3 or 4 kids starring a hole thru me, my Goose was cooked! I will never forget, he lunged at me, pulling me up from my desk! I lost my balance and fell backward, and with his firm hold on my sleeve, it tore away from the shoulder of my shirt. He didn't give the strap either; he whacked your knuckles with a pointer which hurt like hell!

Later on my way home, I thought of how I could explain this one! I decided to tell the truth and make him out to seem mean, but to my dismay, she supported him, saying, "Good on him, you must have deserved it".

I don't know how long Mr. Troy taught at St. Augustine's, but he was one of the few Teachers that I respected. At some point later, he would own the Tim Horton's Donut franchise off York Road and Race Horses etc., under his Enterprises Company. Almost 30 years later in life, we crossed paths at an event in Burlington and became friends. He was the Guest of Honor at my 40th Birthday Party. He passed away a few years ago, and I will never forget him.

At St. Augustine's, the School Bus Kids often arrived after us. We Walkers were already in the Class room. I historically associated them with bad breath. Not that mine was any better, but likely because a number of them would come into our Classroom together on those mornings and with them came the rush of morning breath. On snowy days those bright yellow buses were simply too much of a temptation to let go by without launching a volley of snowballs at them.

They usually just kept rolling along though one day, my friend Norman and I scored two direct hits on the windshield of one. It roared to a halt, and the chase was on, the Driver and two bigger Grade 8 Boys hot on our trail. I got caught though Norman initially had got away. The Bus returned me to the school, and there I was in the Principal's Office with Sister Marcella glaring at me. Of course, under interrogation, my memory was guardedly fuzzy; I wasn't sure or guessing who else had thrown a snowball.

Sister Marcella the Principle was to many of us a scary old lady who we affectionately referred to as "Marble Head". She was though an extremely dedicated educator and in the end result successful for many of us. Now a number of you former Goody Two Shoes reading this likely had never seen the strap let alone having had your hands slapped by one. Stern and sadistic like, she slapped my open palms. Being a veteran of the Belt and Ironing Cord thrashings at home, it wasn't so bad, but after she phoned my Mother, I got another thrashing at Home later free of charge. I also have to say that when it came to corporal punishment at school or at Home, I absolutely deserved every whack! Someone on the Bus later squealed on Norman, and he got his strapping the following day.

Did you know the Beach Boys had a song called Marcella, and every time I heard it, I'd think of our Principal Sister. To some folks reading this, corporal punishment might seem barbaric in this day and age, but for some kids, like me, in retrospect, it often was a good thing to keep us in line. In 1984, the Supreme Court of Canada weighed in on the issue and decreed that "the use of the Strap was an unreasonable application of force in the maintenance of classroom discipline". Today challenging students are suspended aka Holiday. I'll leave my opinion about that between my ears but many of the practices of the good ole days had value.

Funny thing, a few years ago, I came across one of those infamous straps in an old Antique Shop. Though I was tempted to leave with it, the cost was rather excessively high for an unpleasant memory, so I left it there.

The Reluctant Runner

So there I was at Parkside High School in 1967 noting that many guys I knew had joined the School's Sports Teams. Graeme McMaster was a Super Star Cross Country Runner and even Norman got involved trying out for the Junior Foot Ball Team. My Father had been heavily involved with Road Racing. He orchestrated the inaugural Dundas Legion Road Race and even managed to bring Johnny Kelly of Boston Marathon Fame to Dundas to participate on September 15, 1952. Johnny Kelly who was a friend of my Father grunted "This one's for Bill" as he crossed the finish line to win the race for my Father who had passed away 7 months earlier.

In discussing High School Sports with my Mother and learning of my Father's involvement it seemed obvious that I should join the Cross Country Team and Run. Boy did we run, in training around and around the Dundas Driving Park which is almost circular and very close to 1/2 a mile around. To be honest, I certainly struggled with breathing and the stamina required and in the end found it somewhat boring. Now after that Park Training tune up over a number of days, I discovered the truth! Cross Country means exactly that, you run no matter what the terrain, thru Woods, mud, rocks, water. Accordingly tripping and falling into mud is a hazard of the sport and I sure did my share leaving my Mother wondering if I had lied and was playing football!

Soon it was time for a Cross Country Meet with another School. It may have been Dundas District or Waterdown High Schools, I don't recall but here is what happened and as you may have noticed so far, could only happen to me. Away we ran up the hill from the Football Field and I was positioned relatively mid pack of the Runners. We actually were on a trail of sorts so it wasn't a difficult route to follow. Through the Heavy Brush we went and soon the elite Runners like Graeme were out of sight. I decided that I would catch up with them and keep their pace so I took off and soon separated myself from the later group of the pack. I ran as fast as I could but they were nowhere to be seen nor did I see anyone behind me. Most Cross Country Races are about 1-2 miles long. I ran along the trail for several minutes and suddenly it broke thru the Brush into the open and there I was alone running towards the Finish Line across the Football Field. The Coach and a number of other people there started cheering for me. As I ran towards them it suddenly dawned on me that the Runners I had been following were not there and nor were there any behind me!

I had taken a wrong turn someplace and once catching my breath had to tell the Coach who I think was just as embarrassed as I was. I became the laughing stock of the Team and I don't think I finished the year.

Cross Country

Front Row: K. Rose, J. Emeric, R. Waddington, D. Able, P. Atkins, J. Kiely, T. Wright.

Second Row: Mr. Wright, M. Fleming, R. Robinson, M. Langois, R. Kingsbury, R. Donovan, A. Benvenuti.

Third Row: G. Mcmaster, R. Patterson, R. Mckay, D. Kolenski, J. Sibley, A. Duffin, W. Forn.

Chapter Six

The Homestead

Our old Melville Street House in the Heritage District of Dundas was built in the late 1840's. Canada had yet to become a Country then, and Horses pulling Buggies and Wagons navigated the muddy streets. The Industrial, residential area of Dundas was along Hatt Street, and King Street of course was our commercial residential area. Worker's Cottages were added later.

The Cross Street neighborhood became the location of choice for the more prominent Dundas citizens who built substantial residences in the fashion of the time. Most homes in this area date from 1840 to 1890 and, of course, include the original Grafton and Bertram Homes on the Cross Street Hill. Grafton's (1853) was an early and well-known Clothing Store, while John Bertram was one of Dundas's Industrial Founders (1863), The former Knox Presbyterian Church in the east section of Melville Street, was built in 1847 and was restructured in 1875, becoming the local parish. What was known as the 1st Methodist Church stood originally at King and Ogilvie Streets, where the Carnegie Carnegie-financed Library was built many years later.

In 1855, a new Methodist Church was built at Cross and Park Streets, funded by the Ancaster Anglican, St. Augustine's Roman Catholic Church and area Businessmen. This would later become St. Paul's United. In this area, St. Augustine's Church was the earliest being established in a wooden structure in 1827 which burned down and was rebuilt as it sits today in 1863.

Our former Homestead, as you pass by, looks like a small cottage, though it is built on the side of that slope that runs from Cross Street to Sydenham. At the back, you can appreciate the real size of it, given the large bottom section with its entrance off Sydenham Street. Given the slope, when you went out the back door, it was a second-story veranda-like platform featuring a long staircase to the lower level.

In one corner of the kitchen stood a Wringer Washing Machine with those rollers, which I learned later were called "Mangles," used to wring the water out of the clothes. I was fortunate not to get my hands caught in them which was a hazard of the day for many kids back then. I remember my mother kept a stick by the machine to put in the rollers when necessary for safety reasons.

Today, of course, modern washing machines have the spin cycle, which is a vastly superior way to remove excess water from the clothes.

Many windows in the house had what I called wavy glass in them, not unlike a Fun House, they were clear, but when you leaned towards them to look out, it was a distorted view. With the Quebec Heater Coal Stove in the Living Room and a smaller one in the kitchen, we were never uncomfortable in the colder weather, but as with any old house, if it was often drafty and the upstairs was only warmed by whatever heat rose up the stairway.

In the winter, when it got really cold outside, you could scratch out your name on the then then-frosted glass windows. The floors, I presume, were basic pine, somewhat rough and had been covered with linoleum. I only wore socks occasionally to bed, and when your bare feet touched that floor first thing on a winter morning, that jolt helped wake you up. Snuggled in, though, in flannelette Sheets and a Comforter, only your Nose got chilled. Our Pillow Cases were made from boiled Sugar Bags with the still faintly readable brand and they were quite comfortable. My Brother and I would run downstairs in the morning and huddle, almost touching the stoves to warm ourselves up.

I learned later, too, that there wasn't an exactly square room anywhere in the house, as if whoever had built it had laid it out by eye. I remember laying carpet, and when I got to the corner, nothing was square! No Drywall anywhere either, it had yet to be invented when our House was constructed. Everything was plaster, and one morning we really got to appreciate that! It was a weekend morning, and I sat with my Mother, having breakfast in the kitchen. Suddenly there was this horrendous crash which that shook the entire House, coupled with a hair hair-rising scream from upstairs, where my Sister was still sleeping.

My Mother rushed up the stairs with me following, and at the top, we encountered a wild woman covered in plaster dust still screaming. We quickly reversed our course now with the 3 of us running down the stairs. What had happened was a huge chunk of plaster dropped from the Ceiling, striking the bottom of my Sister's Bed and literally catapulting her up in the air!! Later we found a piece of an old newspaper in the plaster dated 1862!

Fast forward to 1974, and my Wife and I are visiting my Mother, now living alone in the House. As we sat in the Kitchen with a coffee, the room suddenly trembled with a very loud thumping noise emanating from the ceiling. We all look at each other, and she says, "Oh, Oh yes, I think I might have a squirrel up there". Squirrel! It sounded like the Tiger Cat Football Team to me! So we go out down the street and around the corner on to Sydenham Street, where we can clearly see the roof at the rear of the House. There sitting on the peak of the roof, is a Momma Raccoon and 4 little ones.

Chapter Seven

Pranks Aplenty

My Sister's first marriage was, unfortunately, a rather short affair, and she returned Home for a period of time. That larger Bedroom I had briefly enjoyed all to myself abruptly changed as a second bed was added for her. My suffering commenced almost immediately. My lights-out was scheduled around 10 p.m., and I was usually fast asleep within the first half hour. Then around 11:30, she would waltz from an afternoon shift at the Dofasco Steel Company, where she worked. The light on the wall above her Bed went on, and she'd cuddle up with her stack of "True Confessions" and "Modern Romances". The combination of the light, squeaky bed springs and pages turning was tortuous, and I'd now be wide awake! As if that wasn't bad enough, there would be more suffering to come! She would then flatter me, saying how nice it was to be sharing a room with me and wouldn't it be fun for her and I to have a midnight snack! Great fun, and, of course, I would get to make it! So there I was, the first time creeping slowly down the stairs, then with my back against the wall, I'd inch my way along it, past the Sergeant Major's Bedroom.

Once I arrived in the Kitchen, it would be a stealth stealth-like operation of combining Peanut Butter and Bread Slices together as quickly and quietly as possible, then slowly making my way back up the hall to the stairs. I am sure a Cat Burglar Instruction Manual would provide advice on how to quietly sneak up 113 year -year-old wooden stairs! In any case, I never made it past the 3rd stair, which creaked loudly, followed by the roar, "Who's up?" While Peanut Butter is reasonably sticky, it wasn't enough to keep the crudely made sandwiches on the plate, and my footprint was easily distinguishable on a stair a few steps up. The evidence, of course, would clearly implicate me, and I would be found guilty regardless of the truth of the matter!

After the tirade settled, I tried to get back to sleep and had plenty of time to plot my revenge! In order to be successful in combat, I had once read you need to study and determine your opponent's weakness! Ah, yes, my sister had a mortal fear of snakes! It may have been Pinder's Five and Dime Dime-like Store in Dundas where I found a very realistic rubber snake made of a very life-like neoprene.

To add to its realism, I hid it in the Fridge first, then gave it a good rubdown with Vaseline. About an hour before she got home, I put it in the bed down near the bottom between sheets, carefully smoothing the blankets again.

Now, she was home and coming up the stairs, and I lay with my head turned away, listening to the squeaky springs, and covers gently rustling. There was a moment of silence followed by a loud gasp, I suspect from the feel of it. I lay there holding my Nose, trying not to make a sound as a loud scream followed, and out the doorway and down the stairs she went. During the subsequent uproar downstairs, I jumped from my bed, grabbed the snake and quickly threw it out the window!

As I recall the scene now, it would have been hilarious to watch had I not anticipated being in trouble. My Sister perched behind my Mother, screaming, "He did it," as Mother gingerly lifted the sheets with a broom handle, searching for the serpent. In retrospect, I might have gotten away with it had I not opted to enhance the reptile with Vaseline, which marked the sheets. Another weekend grounding, though it was worth it

Being of Irish Heritage, one St. Patrick's Day, I discovered some history on Irish Knights, which brought back some memories of long long-ago Dundas Knights. I am not really sure what started a medieval craze of sorts one summer in the early 60's with some of us Dundas kids. There were a number of us, Eddie Mahony, Norman Ragg, Marty Zuliniak and others whose names escape me now.

With our limited carpentry skills, we crafted wooden swords, and shields and created a few helmets too. These crude creations were also often adorned with a bright paint. During this time, a small metal waste basket mysteriously disappeared from my Bedroom, much to my Mother's bewilderment. Taking an old can opener, I fashioned eye hole slits and stuffed an old towel in it for padding. In my mind, it was the Black Knight's frightening Helmet. Well, okay, it did have a few pink flowers on it, but still, it was black, and I thought it intimidating! However, in my first battle wearing it, I failed to significantly frighten the enemy and absorbed a direct blow to my head. My no longer Fearsome Helmet crumpled, and though I survived, my head featured a large goose egg for a number of days.

Eddie lived on King Street West in a House across the street from his Father's Law Office. In a back laneway behind the House was a large two two-story red brick garage of sorts with a second-floor loft. This became a mighty Castle worth battling for. It still stands today just across from the Laundromat of the alleyway on Church Street. Not unlike the historic struggles between the French and English, the Castle's Battlements changed hands several times over the summer.

For these particular Knights, there were no Damsels to rescue either, in fact, they were not even allowed on the premises! In the end, though, the casualty count mounted with a number of unplanned visits to local Doctors (very few kids ever went to a hospital in those days). Some Knights battle gear was confiscated in lieu of more peaceful playtimes, and life went on.

Though getting whacked with a wooden sword was painful, to be sure, a lesser weapon of choice, too, was the Catapult. Our basic design was a larger rock or railway tie and a 1 X 6 Fence Board. Down the Street from my old House stands the Knox Presbyterian Church. The original Manse was located across the street. Reverend Walter Allum and his Family lived there. Reverend Allum was a well-loved and respected Minister in our neighborhood. I sometimes played with his Children, Nancy, Mary and young John, and as you'll see, was likely not considered a positive influence. On this day, I had taken my Fence Board over to their house and commenced to show John the intricacies of a catapult.

The firing mechanism was pretty basic; you set the middle of the board down on a larger rock and/or railway tie tie-like board. Then you placed a mud ball or other projectile on one end then stomped your foot down on the other. In battle, mud balls were far less dangerous but not appreciated by your enemy either. So I fired a few demonstration like volleys against the light-colored siding at the rear of the Manse. As we stood back admiring the artful design, out the door roared Reverend Allum, who did not appreciate the artwork! By the seat of my pants, he marched me up the street to knock at our front door! My sincere hope that no one would be home was dashed as my Mother opened the door. Speaking of Castles and such, I did end up in a dungeon of sorts for a number of days.

A number of years later, there was another knock on the front door of our house, and there stood another Man of the Cloth. I had married in the early 70's and moved away from Dundas. My Mother, living alone by then, looked out on one of those former Knights of Old, now Father Edward Mahony. Eddie had joined the Priesthood and just dropped by to see how I was doing. Father Mahony was recently the Pastor of Our Lady of Mount Carmel Church in Freelton, Ontario but is now retired living in St. Elizabeth Village on the West Hamilton Mountain.

How many of you can remember the term back in the day, "Calling on Kids?" I remember Kids coming over to my House and/or going over to theirs to get together to play. Thinking back, we seldom knocked or rang a Doorbell. I'd be in the House, and I would hear, "Allan Oh Allan" from outside, or if I didn't, my Mother would say your Friends are here. So you went outside to meet them. I remember my friend Norman always slept in on the weekends, so an outside call to his House wasn't possible. I'd knock at the front door, but his Mother, upon answering, would always say, "he's still sleeping".

That used to bug me as at my house, the Drill Sergeant (Mother) would always roust you out of bed at the crack of dawn! Well, it'd be at least 7 o'clock anyway. So, knowing where Norman's Bedroom was on the 2nd floor of his House, when his Mother wasn't cooperating, I would gather up small pebble pebble-like stones from the street and bounce a few off his window. It always worked, after a number of stones; I'd see the shade come up and his tousled hairy head looking out.

No wonder he slept in, he actually had a small TV, B&W, of course as most were then in his room. Just imagine this was before a lot of us even had a TV in the House! On Saturday Nights in the winter, we were allowed to watch Hockey Night in Canada up there. That was back in the day when it didn't come on TV until halfway thru the 1st period. Foster, Son Bill Hewitt and Danny Gallivan were the Play-by-play Guys with Ward Cornell doing between between-period interviews, and who could forget the Esso Gasoline Happy Motoring Commercials with Murray Westgate in his Uniform?

Esso Ad Actor Murray Wesgate

Murray passed away after reaching over 100 years old in 2018.

The Esso Happy Motoring Jingle has never left my memory. I remain a Leaf Fan today, despite their continued torturous shortcomings. Unfortunately for me, Norman was a Montreal Fan, so on some nights, it was a rather tense relationship if either Team was dominating the other. Occasionally, I left, going home early if Montreal was way ahead or was ordered out if the Canadians were taking a drubbing! Outside earlier in the day, with our imaginations on full bore, we would take turns firing Tennis Balls with Hockey Sticks trying to hit the Garage Door while, in our imaginations, a would-be famous Goaltender of that day guarded it. Fortunately, Norman's Parents didn't mind the resulting artwork from the shots that scored bouncing off the Door, leaving a unique design.

Speaking of Hockey Night in Canada and Dundas, let me share another nugget of Dundas's History that some folks might remember. During the late 70's, The Leafs were then an up-and-coming Team with the likes of Darryl Sittler, Borje Salming, Ian Turnbull and others. Long-time Dundasians would certainly remember the Myers Brothers, Bob and Don, who were fixtures on the Dundas Merchants Hockey Team in the 60's. I and a few friends went to a number of games often scoring seats behind the Net. We were often ejected for making unkind remarks about the opposing Team Goalie's Mother.

Bob Myers went on to become a very well-known and respected NHL Referee, and Myers Sports and Cycle was a prominent Dundas King Street Business. It escapes me now who the Leafs were playing one night on Hockey Night in Canada, thinking perhaps, the Philadelphia Flyers, then known as the Broad Street Bullies. In any case, Salming and Inga Hammerstrom were the first Professional Swedish Players to play in the NHL. Salming, arguably one of the all-time great Leaf's Defensemen was a smooth, talented skater.

During a rather testy game, he was jumped by another Player and was, in the opinion of many, unfairly penalized by Myers. Salming was so incensed he took his stick and made it seem like he was going to swing it at Myers. He didn't, of course, but Myers ducked and then gave him a game misconduct, ejecting him from the game. Later that night in Dundas, a disgruntled Leaf Fan threw a Brick thru the Front Window of Myer's Sports and Cycle! Likely someone reading this knows who the culprit was though for a change, it wasn't me, honest!

Chapter Eight

Hide, Seek & Snacks

Now when you are watching a Sporting Event, Peanuts or Popcorn are absolute necessities! Back in the day before Orville Redenbacher's Popping Corn or Microwaves were invented, there were two popular Popcorn Brands, TV Time and Jiffy. Both were Kid Friendly to a degree.

Jiffy Pop was created by a Guy named Frederick Mennen in 1958 and still exists today! You just slid the frying pan like an aluminum disc back and forth over the burner and watched the silver ball that quickly expanded! Remember the jingle, "As much fun to make as it is to eat!"

Though it was definitely more fun to make, I could never qualify as a Connoisseur of Popcorn, though in my humble opinion, I always thought the TV Time tasted better. As kids, we'd grab a pot, squeeze in the oil from one side of the package, pour in the corn kernels, and once the popping started starts, just keep sliding the pot back and forth and wait for the popping to finish.

Many a cold winter Saturday night, we popped and wolfed it down watching the Hockey Game. Another historic Dundas moment was one night when the large glass bowl slipped off the bed, hitting the floor and shattering with a loud crash of glass. I will never forget the anguished wail that erupted from Norman's Mother downstairs, "My Salad Bowl"! I don't know what the big deal was; Pinders Store had 100's hundreds of them.

As Kids, we all played the classic Hide and Seek Game, and you all know the rules. Someone closes their eyes and counts down while the others wildly scatter and hide! Now I will remind you that my Sister "Can" was 14 years older than me. You know what they say about payback, so after her having to lug me around as a small kid for years, I got my turn. Her oldest Son, Brian, was 6 years my junior and when I was about 12 or so, I often got stuck with him on the occasional weekend. I had to take him everywhere with me.

So there we were over at Norman's House one weekend with nobody home playing Hide and Seek. My Nephew, at my instruction, quickly followed me, and we headed for the basement. It was a creepy place and gloomy with the lights out. In those shadows, there was an Octopus-like Oil Furnace and a large Coffin-like Freezer. A perfect hiding place, so I opened the Freezer lid and had my Nephew climb in.

Quickly closing it, I scampered away, hiding in another far corner. A few minutes later, Norman arrived in the Basement looking about. Unsuccessful at finding us, he turned to leave when the noise started. Muffled yelling and pounding from the Freezer which quickly gave my Nephew's hidden location away. Hearing that I started to laugh and we both were found! Of course, in retrospect, I appreciate the downside of my suggested hiding place, but hey, he never would have found us!! Funny to this day, my Nephew makes a point of telling people I once locked him in a freezer which could have resulted in, well, a different story, and of course, I respond by saying "I should have left him in there".

Chapter Nine

Legendary Explorations

As Spring brings warmer weather, awakening nature each year, I am reminded of our youthful explorations in the area's wilderness. While Dundas was a tidy little town back then, we kids didn't have to venture too far away to escape it and have great wilderness adventures. The Marsh (Cootes Paradise) on the East side of town provided our game fish of the day, Carp and Suckers. While the Marsh could not compete with the Florida Everglades for scary things, there was still an abundance of nasty Snapping Turtles and snakes there too. One day coming home from the Marsh with a cache of snakes, I came up with an idea to surprise my Mother and make her day! She had planted what she called "Snake Plants" in pots on either side of the front doorstep.

Thinking how surprised and happy she would be, I put a Garter Snake in each plant. Later hearing the scream, I knew at least the surprise part had gone over well. I honestly believed I was doing those plants a favor. Not quite, I guess, as I had to get rid of two perfectly good snakes and was "grounded" for the rest of the day though I suppose it could have been worse.

Now for a change of pace on different days, we headed for the Mountain, and where we lived, you had to travel first through the Old Canada Crushed Stone Quarry. That place on its own could provide hours of entertainment, especially crawling along its boxed-in conveyor beltline.

I am not sure what the Dundas Museum might have recorded, but in the center of the Quarry was a butte of sorts containing an old cemetery, and they had simply dug around it for the stone. I remember seeing the broken headstones and hearing Urban Legends about various bones being discovered there by kids. Today, of course, that area boasts a subdivision where the Quarry used to be. Likely solid foundations for those Homes.

But for a true adventure, you had to climb higher past the Quarry to come across Mackenzie's Cave and a large pond near it. William Lyon Mackenzie led the Upper Canada Rebellion in 1837, and area legend purports in stayed in this Dundas area cave while being pursued by Government Forces on his way to Niagara Falls. As he had a force of 200 men with him, if he did, it must have been quite crowded!

Mackenzie's Cave

There is controversy on where Mackenzie's Cave actually was, but for us, it was absolutely by the pond. It was a large Karst-like opening in the rock with some small passages you could crawl through. The location in question became a Landfill site in later years; hence no longer exists.

Mackenzies's Cave Photo Dundas Museum and Archives

Just inside the entrance was a Fire Pit of sorts where I am sure 100's of Kids had burned wieners on a stick or tried to dry their wet clothes. Some youthful explorers from earlier times had built a rather crude raft which we poled across the pond. Someone invariably fell in, getting soaked. It was a long, miserable hike back home in such a condition.

Up on a hill, a ways from the Cave, stood a stand of Pine Trees. With too much competition for the Cave Fire Pit one day, my friend Norman and I made a campsite up there. We learned about putting a can of beans in the coals of a fire to heat them. While anyone could take bologna or peanut butter sandwiches on their adventure, Beans or Hot Dogs cooked over a fire were quite authentic to us. One day with a sound I would describe as a loud 'whump," the Beans went everywhere, covering us and the nearby trees. We, not quite seasoned explorers, had neglected to poke a hole in the can, and it exploded!

Lastly was the trek up thru the Ravine to Webster's Falls and/or the now-famous Dundas Peak. Though we fished up there in the creek a number of times, we were never successful at catching anything though I do remember watching Trout in a deep pool there.

My earliest adventures in that area were with Marty Zuliniak and other Kids, and we indeed discovered a Hobo Camp, originally a large Pit with a makeshift roof over it. There was a ladder to climb down. There we found a large bag of potatoes stashed for a future meal. The proximity of the railway tracks, coupled with the Hobo travel of the day, made the Ravine a popular camp location. Now once into the Ravine, when we really thirsted for adventure, we would explore further, following a pathway up thru it to the far end where at a clearing, we would come upon the bottom of Webster's Falls. On particularly hot days off would come our clothes, save for underwear, and we would frolic in a small pool at the bottom of the Falls. There were old rickety metal stairs at the side, which always scared me. They would sway slightly as you climbed up them to enter the park above.

While Websters, Tews and Borers Falls are considered Dundas features, a number of years ago, the City of Hamilton, Ontario, which now includes Dundas was christened as the City of Water Falls given our significant Escarpment. With it came hordes of Tourists and a nightmare for many local residents residing near these natural wonders. Garbage and, in some neighborhoods, a sea of cars parked along roadways, blocking driveways etc. Those streets in question are now heavily patrolled by Bylaw Enforcement who dole out expensive Tickets for illegal parking. As well, the trails to these area geographic wonders that we played in as kids require Reservation and Paid Entry Tickets. As Grand Parents this is a hard reality for many of us to accept now for our local kids and Families.

As for the Ravine, in the late 60's, Marty Zuliniak gained his fame as he returned there conducting the then-infamous Ravine Bashes, which were basically youthful drinking parties. These celebrations were Cat and Mouse like affairs where the local Police, eventually figured out the date though but were tasked to find the location and were reinforced with Ontario Provincial Police.

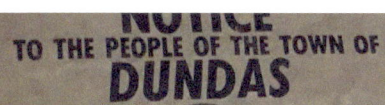

NOTICE
TO THE PEOPLE OF THE TOWN OF
DUNDAS

There are overt elements of subversion making Dundas unfit for dwelling.
They are defeating the purpose of a home.
They have caused the downfall of local government.
They are about to render the voice of Dundas worthless.
They have made the name of our town undecipherable.
They are about to cause this name to be forgotten.
They have demolished the House of Providence.
They are about to obliterate the Resurrection Novitiate.
They are promoting injury to Leonard's factory.
They are dilapidating the Elgin House block.
They have hurt the Fire Hall.
They have destroyed Memorial Square.
They have blotted out Desjardin's Canal.
They are about to wreck the Cotton Mill.
They have scarred the mountain while ruining Sydenham hill.
They have damaged every scenic entrance to The Valley.
They are selling our healthy walnut trees to the U.S.S.A.
They have injured the main streets with wide pavement & the murder of trees.
They are defacing us with highway-robbery, highrise-robbery & other forms of vandalism.
They are about to plunder the train station, & the Post Office, & the open spaces on York & Governor's Roads.
They are about to plunder what little remains.
They are... ad nauseum...

They have effected the transference of local traditions.
They, themselves, are local traditions.
BUT DESPAIR NOT:
They are NOT about to erase local traditions themselves.

DO YOU FIND THE STREETS OF YOUR TOWN NOT WORTH WALKING?
OF COURSE YOU DO, SO...

COME TO!
THE SEVENTH
ANNUAL RAVINE BASH
JUNE '73
A REAL TREAT
A DUNDAS TRADITION

Over a friendly beer, express to your neighbours your desire to see Dundas secede from Ontario...
Under a friendly table, discuss with your fellow townfolk the desirability of Dundas rejoining Quebec.

ALL YOU CAN DRINK
for the modest admission fee of $4.00
DOOR PRIZES. CONTESTS. AWARDS. COLDER BEER. AND MORE.
The Committee humbly regrets to inform the public they cannot be responsible for lost persons.

TICKETS ON SALE NOW   ONLY IN DUNDAS
Everyone Welcome. Try to be eighteen.

A CELEBRATION IN HONOUR OF THE MEMORY OF THE TOWN OF DUNDAS
WITH GREAT EXPECTATIONS FOR THE FUTURE.
"May the Dundas cannon never be used, save for the rejoicing days."

DUNDAS
CANADA

DUNDAS. CANADA.
Summer of June, 1973.

I missed attending those infamous classic parties having worked summer relief at a Hamilton Hospital. Marty Zuliniak was the Son of John Zuliniak with siblings as shown here, Terry, Billy, Marty, David, John (Dad) Lora Lynn, Rose (Mom) and Jean.

John Zuliniak was a well-respected Dundas Town Councilor running successfully for two terms in the 60's and 70's. Later on, in the mid-70s thru early 80's, Marty would again rise in notoriety in fronting the Rhinoceros Party running for Mayor and Council in Dundas and the City of Hamilton on a number of occasions.

His involvement, while genuinely satirical, provided great entertainment in otherwise dull elections.

Boys scampering thru all those wilderness adventures once back home required significant clearing. We had one Bathroom in our old House, and it was located in the interior with no external window. It did have though what is called a Transom Window above the Door. That window was always open a crack, presumably to allow steam and other fragrances to escape the bathroom. It was small as bathrooms go, with a claw foot bathtub, toilet and a small sink. It allowed for the basics, once you sat on the Toilet, your knees would be almost touching the side of the tub. Two people in there would be a crowd.

Another of my Mothers oft declared Mantras was "Cleanliness is next to Godliness". While that sounds admirable, as a young boy, I only had a bath on Sundays unless an event otherwise dictated it. I like playing in the brine barrels behind Strub's Pickle's original location beside Walker's Hardware. I'd come home reeking of Dill Pickles but deny I'd ever been near the place. I provide the bathroom dimensions as a possible reason why I suffered a scrubbing 6 nights a week at the kitchen sink. Just before bedtime, I'd be summoned there for my "neck and ears" to be washed. My Mother was a cleanliness zealot who I swore was wearing my skin away with her vigorous scrubbing.

When she washed your hair, it was worse, her fingernails gouging your scalp, and it may have assisted my eventual receding hairline. Then you'd have to stand or pull up a chair and stick your head over the kitchen coal stove for a while to dry your hair as the only Hair Dryers then were in Beauty Salons. I remember sitting there listening to CHML Radio shows like 'The Shadow'.

To be honest, I don't think I've ever had a bath since I left that House in Dundas. Being scrunched up in a tub with dirty, soapy water is not my idea of getting clean. I couldn't imagine not starting each day since then with a shower, and, yes, my Neck and Ears, as identified by my Mother, remain one of the cleaning priorities.

Today as I experience a thunderstorm, I am often reminded of a Duffin Family drill as a child. With the distant rumble of an approaching Storm, the Drill was to get off the telephone immediately, run and unplug appliances with the Television as the 1st priority and get away from the windows. I also recall being yanked out of the Bathtub!

At St. Augustine's School, I remember Mrs. Denomme, my Grade 4 Teacher telling us occasionally terrified kids to put our heads down on our desk tops as a Spring Thunder Storm roared and banged thru the Valley. As I got older later, the foregoing to me was akin to "Old Wives Tales," but in researching this, I was surprised to learn the following. The above-noted practices continue to be recommended to this day, and Dundas is much safer than Florida, considered to be the Lightning Capital of North America. Over 2,000 people have been injured or killed by Lightning strikes in Florida over the past 50 years, who knew!?

In the early 1960's, the Dundas P.U.C made the bold decision to light up the Town! It was quite the sensation at the time, and it was claimed that Dundas would be the most brightly lit Town, east of Las Vegas! Note in the photos displayed here, the daytime and evening look of the fixtures and their brightness.

Dundas Museum and Archives

Also, in this Evening Photo, you can see both the original street lights and the glaring brilliance of the newer lights. The new lights at that time appear in this photo to be 4-foot-long fluorescent fixtures which did provide quite a swath of brightness to the downtown. While progress and innovation are exciting, for me now, I am glad the downtown look has been refitted with it's original lighting, which many of us remember as Kids and, when enhanced at Christmas, provides a beautiful Streetscape.

Chapter Ten

The Dump

Today as you walk or drive along the streets of your neighborhood on Garbage Day, you will see tidy rows of Green Bins, Plastic Garbage Bags and Blue Recycling Boxes. If you are in the vicinity of the Garbage Truck, perhaps following it allows a street on a hot summer's day; there is no mistaking of that unique scent. In my brain, I can't decipher what it smells like other than simply "garbage", a smell of its own.

Back in the day in Dundas, like any other Town, on Garbage Day, it was a much different streetscape. Jumbled piles of trash of various descriptions and metal garbage cans, often overflowing, littered the sidewalk curbs. That strong, unique smell wafting through the air was unmistakable, though and as young boys, we didn't find it that bad. To us, the best thing about garbage was that it often yielded incredible treasures!

The Sheeny Man certainly knew! For those who might not recall those characters, it was a man who slowly trundled along in his wagon with the Horse's hooves, a clopping even well into the 50's. "Rags, Bottles," he'd chant, and Folks would set out such things, including newspapers. To be totally honest here, while I certainly recall seeing the Sheeny Man, Horse and all, I can't swear that it was in Dundas. Likely in the then nearby City of Hamilton while there with my Mother shopping. I am sure many will remember him regardless of the location.

My initial experience with Metal Garbage Pails was retrieving and refilling them from the bottom of our back stairs courtesy of our evening raccoon visitors. No matter how many bricks or other heavy items we placed on the lids, they never failed at knocking them over, spreading a sumptuous buffet down the stairs.

Though I watched the Garbage Men come along emptying our trash cans into the truck, the thought of where it went to never occurred to me. It was strictly by accident one day that while coming home from the nearby Marsh, my Friend Norman and I came upon this wondrous site! Huge mounds of the most fascinating objects of every description! Yes, it was a bit yucky here and there with, of course, that pungent garbage smell, but if you carefully waded through it, you could find really neat stuff! Unfortunately, when you brought that neat stuff home, the familiar odor came with you. Like the Strubs Pickle Brine Barrels, those odors wrecked whatever alibi you could come up with when lying about where you had really been. God only knows what toxic liquids we splashed thru in that dump back then in search of treasures.

There was one unique Dump experience that I'd like to share with you. I wonder as well if anyone reading this may have unwittingly played a part in an experience that follows. One Fall Weekend, we had been fishing in the Marsh in the late afternoon on a Saturday, and darkness was well on its way. Stopping at the dump as usual to have a look around, we spied a Car parked well in among the mountainous piles of trash. Wondering what a Car could be in there for, we snuck up to have a look. We couldn't believe our luck, there they were, two Teenagers making out. I don't think we watched long before one of us decided to toss a stick at the Car. It hit with a resounding thump, and like Gophers, two heads reared up quickly. This was followed by a frantic discussion, and then the Car roared out of the Dump as we stood there in hysterics.

Chapter Eleven

The Sailor

Many of my vintages will remember that in our day, it was our imagination and not PlayStations that fueled our fun and entertainment. Young girls took care of their Dolls and conducted Tea Parties while we boys had our adventures as Cowboys in the old West, Knights of Old or attacking enemy soldiers from the not so long before War!

A few years later and now as teenagers, for boys, it became much more real, and there would be Uniforms, real weapons and strict discipline! Well, maybe not exactly for my group though more on that later. There were a number of military-like options available to us for real adventure!! Dundas had Sea Cadets, and the Armed Forces Militia, and there were Air Cadets too, though, with the absence of an immediate plane ride, the Air Force didn't interest me.

It was initially the Sea Cadets that got my attention, quite likely because my older Brother Billy had joined the Navy at 18 and later saw service on the HMCS Lauzon, a Supply Frigate.

Billy, Mom and Allan and Allan as Sea Cadet

Those who lived in Dundas back then will remember a small Ship that sat by the Desjardin's Canal and could be clearly seen from 102 Hwy (Cootes Drive). It was part of the landscape of Dundas for close to 20 years. Here is a bit of her history.

In 1957, the Motor Launch Q-104, (COUGAR), a Fairmile Ship, arrived in Dundas from the Hamilton Star and became the training facility for the Dundas Sea Cadets. This Ship was originally built in Sarnia and delivered to the Canadian Navy in early August of 1943. Her wartime service was providing Escort duty from the mouth of the St. Lawrence River into the Atlantic Ocean and later 600 miles off

New York City patrolling around Bermuda, a member of the British Commonwealth.

Photo B. Kevin Joint

The Farmile "Cougar"

It was originally manned by a compliment complement of 14 Sailors and 2-3 Officers. Many of these Ships, when in original service, were typically armed with 20 MM Guns and Depth Charges. They forged a stellar reputation as "Fighting Little Ships" who successfully harassed and disrupted Germany's Atlantic U Boat Fleet probing Canada's shores and torpedoing Supply Ships. A general overview follows here, but there is quite detailed information on Fairmiles which can be found online.

Fairmiles were renowned for their speed, given their lightweight wooden hulls. As Metal was in short supply then, these Motor Launches were constructed of double mahogany at a length of 116 feet. They were powered by 650 to 700 horse horse-powered engines that allowed a speed beyond that of comparably sized ships in the British Navy. The photo shown here is the Dundas Q104 while in actual service. By the time she reached Dundas, the original Engine Room had been gutted and replaced with a Furnace to warm her interior. I remember her well having a hatch hatch-like opening with a steel ladder near the Bow, and the main hatchway near the Aft to the lower deck had a stairway. There was a unique canvas canvas-like smell to her interior, and anyone who ever went in it will surely remember it. I recall during my tenure as a Sea Cadet painting her the battleship grey colour at least twice on platforms and scaffolding-like configurations around her Hull.

A little ditty I created to remember the naval terms of the sides of the ships went, "The Starboard Side is on the right and Port on the left of this floating Fort". Those descriptions identify the right and left sides of a ship when looking forward to its Bow. They were established way back in time and are an interesting read on their own which you can google. Next came the Boatswain, you know, that different whistle sound that is blown when they raised or lowered the flag or an important announcement is made to the crew, "Now Here This".

The Sea Cadet Uniform was a Naval Naval-like standard that most folks would be familiar with. The cold weather coats were black and called Great Coats and were made from heavyweight wool. Though quite heavy to wear, they did keep you incredibly warm in the winter. I mention the weight of that coat here because, with a surge of adrenalin, it felt like light nylon one night.

I was briefly seeing a young lady who lived on a nearby street. One evening after Sea Cadets, I decided to pay her a visit and a shipmate of mine, George Taylor, walked along part of the way with me. Here we were, taking a shortcut thru the Grove Cemetery for me to get over to her Street and George to go home. It was a cold winter's night with a full moon, and you could see your breath as we walked along. Eerily quiet as a Cemetery should be at that time, we suddenly heard what was an obvious sound and stopped to listen. It was a sound which that I swear to this day was like someone digging up something! I don't remember who bolted first, but it was a Marathon of sorts as we tore out of there their heavy great coats and all, terrified.

Later on, after I had left the Sea Cadets, one night, Norman and I went down there to the Ship and snuck on board in the dark, and we hoisted our crude version of a former enemy flag from WW2 up her Flagpole as a prank.

Chapter Twelve

The Funeral Home

Looking back, my first experience with death was with a pet Hamster. While I don't recall its name nor where it came from, it was certainly not from my Mother, who was not an Animal Lover. It resided in a cage on the floor of our Kitchen and got out once, to my Mother's horror, skittering around with its newfound freedom.

Already being terrified of mice and all the small furry-like creatures who scurried about, for my Mother, the experience was unbearable. Assuming her famous Mouse stance up on a chair, she waited until it was caught and put back in the cage. It was a cold winter day, but she demanded it be put out on the back porch. While I did my best to provide some extra insulation, the following morning, it had passed and was frozen stiff! I was heartbroken, and because the ground was too hard for a graveside service, it was put out with the trash.

Back in the 50's and 60's, there were two Funeral Homes in Dundas. Marlatt's, as it remains to this day, is uptown near today's Lions Club Hall and the other, Cattel & Eaton, was downtown across from the old Town Hall. At differing times, we played in the vicinity of both Funeral Homes. I always found them creepy and bathed in the urban legends of the day, which for kids, was the absolute truth! Over the years, there have been differing opinions regarding children, their understanding of death and whether they should be allowed to visit the deceased in Funeral Homes.

As an Adult, my career was in EMS for 42 years, and I certainly had my share of death experiences. However, based on my own experiences as a child, my humble opinion follows. I maintain that the maturity level of a child must be carefully considered when determining their level of involvement with the deceased where

Funeral Homes are involved. In many cases, an explanation would be sufficient as opposed to exposing a child to what might be a frightening observation.

I recall my Brother who, as a young teenager, experienced the sudden death of a Classmate as a result of a hunting accident. Fortunately for me, being much younger at the time, I was not involved with the subsequent funeral experience. My Brother had previously gone on local hunting expeditions with two friends. One day for whatever reason, he could not join them as they took rifles and went up through the Ravine near the Dundas Peak.

On the way down, while climbing during an exchange, a shotgun they were carrying went off, striking one of the boys. His terrified friend carried him down the mountain and over to a Doctor's office, but he had passed. As my Brother tells it, my Mother, of course, made him go with her to the Funeral Home. He viewed his deceased friend and hardly recognized him. He heard later from my Mother that his friend's Mother had wanted the Casket to be left open so that all of the kids attending could see the result of playing with firearms!

My first experience with someone that I had known was a few years later when my Mother took me to the Convent off the York Road in Dundas to view a former Nun School Principal. There she lay in this black black-clothed box. Though I recognized her, no cosmetics had been applied, and the fact she was no longer alive was clearly evident. I had nightmares for weeks.

Throughout her life, my Mother felt strongly that our family should always pay their respects at Funeral Services for Family, Friends and others she thought appropriate. A short while after the Convent experience, a local friend of mine was involved in a tragic accident where on his bicycle, he was run over by a large Soft Drink Truck downtown near the Post Office. He died and later I was taken to the downtown Funeral Home and once again was positioned front and center, viewing someone who kind of looked familiar but was significantly different too. Once more, a succession of nightmares followed.

There were a number of other scenarios too thereafter into my teenage years, including being a Pall Bearer. George and Kenneth Taylor and a Friend lost their lives in a horrific car accident. I will never forget accepting this solemn responsibility which was nonetheless a very sad and uncomfortable experience. As I helped carry George to his final resting place, the popular Beatles song of the day, "All You Need is Love," played between my Ears, though I needed and wished for so much more..

At some point, my Mother appointed my older Sister Carole to be our Family Emissary in Funeral Home visits. Daily she would gather the newspaper up off the doorstep and page directly to the Obituary Section, announcing, "I wonder who's dead". When I heard the phrase "Oh, Dear poor Mr. or Mrs. so, and so". I knew we would soon be on our way to another uncomfortable experience someplace.

I made those trips with my Sister well into my 20's, offering condolences on behalf of our family, mostly to people who I didn't know or remember! In many cases, it was Folks who my Mother had not seen for years. Much to my chagrin, the phrase "Oh, you're little Allan" was a common greeting and indicative of the number of years before when they had last seen me.

For many years my Sister was also the official monitor of the Family's Grave Stone perpetual care agreements, notifying the Cemeteries when stones required raising. I have now inherited this responsibility. My Parents and Sister's Graves are in Burlington while David Hood and Uncle Gord rest in the Dundas Grove, each being about a 100 feet from my Aunt and Uncle, Gladys and Tommy Heugh and Cousin Lois, our original upstairs Tenants in our Melville Street Home.

For me, I am glad that the practice of putting those who have passed on display in a parlor for several days is no longer a frequent occurrence. I think we would all choose to remember people as they were while living. It always seemed Gladiolas were the Flower of choice though I only knew them as Funeral Home Flowers. Today I can't visit a Flower Shop or Show and inhale the scented fragrance without an immediate rush of Funeral Home memories. When my time comes, I have asked not to have a Fish Photo in my obituary and to be returned and scattered in a well known Dundas location.

Chapter Thirteen

Old Dundas Stores

Laing's Grocery Store in Dundas was established by Peter and Robert Laing and first appeared in a rebuilt section of King Street in Dundas after a fire in 1892. Their new Building was stylishly constructed of Italianate Design with ornate window detailing; it remains in excellent condition today and was the backdrop of a recent Ontario Lottery TV Commercial. I imagine those Apartments above are significantly larger than today's standards.

Laing's Grocery Store circa 1900

Photo Dundas Museum and Archives

The Laing Brothers were prominent Dundas Grocers, and the Family Business continued there for 76 years from 1892 until 1968. My Brother, recently being scheduled for a Medical Appointment, was surprised at the address being near 13 King Street, West which he recalled as the Laing's Grocery Store location of his youth. George Laing and his Brother Walter were the Sons of one of the aforementioned Laing Brothers, and they were the Proprietors of Laing's Grocery which continued thru 1950's and early 60's. George managed the store while Walter was the Bee Keeper who provided the Store's Honey from Hives located at the Rear of the Store.

My Brother Billy was one of many Boys who worked for George Laing as a Delivery and Stock Boy. He delivered groceries on his bicycle in brown paper bags, which have come full circle now being in vogue once again today. He recalls that when grocery orders were received, if an item Laing's did not carry was on the list, my Brother would be sent to Piccone's, the nearby Fruit and Vegetable Store, for it. Mr. Laing would carefully remove their price label and reaffix his own to the item.

While working for Mr. Laing, my Brother often came home with a Cereal Box or two of what was considered to be a stale product. We would be excited to open the box to search and find the prize inside. My Mother would then determine if the Cereal was still edible and if not, it went in the garbage.

You might be surprised to know that it was actually Al Capone who had a hand in how product dating was originally established in the 1930's when he lobbied the Chicago City Council to introduce milk dating after a relative became ill from drinking spoiled milk. Presumably, back then, removing a possible stale product was at the whim of the storekeeper based on how long it had been on the shelf. The best-before dates that we see on products today were actually introduced in the early 1970's.

I remember our Cereal of the day back then was a huge bag of puffed wheat, and for a while, they actually had a small glass in them you could collect. Sheriff's Pudding Packages featured plastic Hockey Coins, and I also remember the Cartoon Glasses, which featured the painted characters on them and were filled with Peanut Butter. We had a number of such glasses from the Disney Epic, Cinderella, which were issued in the mid-50's. Who could forget the Margarine Bag with the red dot you broke to spread the colour? That was often my job to massage that bag for an hour or so. Later on, my Mother decided she didn't like the taste, and we switched back to the more expensive Butter.

Speaking of Butter, one day, my Brother recalls, Mr. Laing received a call and a complaint about the taste of the Butter he had sold to a customer. My Brother was sent to retrieve it from a Lady. Back at the store, Mr. Laing carefully unwrapped the end of the butter, reshaped it with a knife, then resealed the package and had my Brother deliver it back. Later the Lady phoned Mr. Laing, saying the replacement butter was the best she had ever tasted. Apparently, she was a bit eccentric.

George Laing often regaled my Brother with stories on quieter Saturday afternoons. Though officially a Delivery and Shelf Stocking Boy, I am sure Mr. Laing also appreciated his company. One time Mr. Laing recanted how his family had once prospected for gold in the Klondike!! He would often recite, word for word, Robert Service's famous Poem, The Shooting of Dan McGrew, a gold rush classic.

The Dundas Museum and Archives retain a number of original items from the Laing's Grocery Store, including some Counters, the Coffee Grinder, pickle/cracker barrels etc. At one time, many years ago, there was a Laing's Grocery Store Display on the lower level of the Museum with the various products of long ago displayed and including a Shop Keepers Mannequin. Though Display space is always a challenge for any Museum, a renewed Laing's Grocery Store display would likely still be a fascinating exhibit for the Museum's patrons today.

Dundas Historical Records show Patrick and Peter Brady, who were Tinsmiths and had immigrated to Canada from Ireland, settling in Dundas around the turn of the century. During the 1950's, it was their heir, Charlie Brady who operated the Tinsmith Shop, on the west side of Walker's Hardware at 59 King Street. Here is his story as told to my Brother by George Laing.

Apparently, Mr. Brady, while carrying on the Tin Smith Business, also sold various stoves and piping pieces, among other things. As Mr. Laing told it, Mr. Brady was a bit odd and often wore the same clothes for many days in a row. The financial transactions for his Tin Shop products and services were conducted from a wad of cash circled with an elastic band from his pants pocket. Mr. Brady resided by himself in an Apartment up over his store.

One day he failed to open his store, and after it had remained closed for a number of days, the Police were contacted to investigate. Charlie Brady was found deceased in his Apartment. After an unsuccessful search locally, a distant relative was finally located in the USA. Arrangements were made to liquidate the estate by conducting an auction of both the contents of the Business and Mr. Brady's personal effects.

As the Auctioneers began to catalogue the items, they discovered several wads of cash hidden here and there inside the stoves. Much of the cash was so old that it actually crumbled as they tried to count it, and the Bank advised that only those bank notes where the serial numbers could be identified could be redeemed. The discovery of these hidden bank notes amounted to a significant find of several thousand dollars. Later on, someone picking at the Town Dump noticed an unusual lump in a mattress from Mr. Brady's residence and found a further large sum totaling thousands more he had stashed there. Obviously, Charlie Brady had a distrust of Banks, keeping his money to himself.

My Brother also remembers that Laing's Grocery and Brady's Tin Shop were the last two stores in Dundas with Gas-lit lights right into the mid 50's. He recalls that when you walked into the store, you could not only smell the gas, but you could actually taste it as well. As long-time Dundas Residents will remember, Walker's Hardware, located between those two businesses' had a reputation for having just about anything you might require. They maintained an incredible stock there with many old items from years gone by still new, like in their original packaging. I still remember as a Kid being fascinated by the sliding ladder they pushed along the floor with the Clerks scampering up them to retrieve stock from the high shelving on the back wall. Today that Building houses the Bridal Salon which still features the original ceilings and sliding ladder.

King Street East, Dundas, Laing's original location

Some of my Brother's other memories of Dundas recall Piconc's Market had a fancy 1966 Turquoise Chevrolet Delivery Truck that was maintained in mint condition for several years.

Piconies Food Market circa 1970

Photo Dundas Museum and Archives

    Guiseppe (Joseph) first came to Canada from Scily in 1911. Unable to find employment in his chosen profession as a Bricklayer he settled in Dundas and began selling fruit door to door. His original Basket is maintained and featured in the Dundas Museum and Archives. The original store location of 1918 at 34 King Street, West continues operating today as Picone's Fine Foods a popular business know for it's quality products and services and is one of Dundas's oldest Business. (Dundas Museum and Archives)

I have my own recollection of Picone's, as I attended St. Augustine's School with a young Paul Picone. Occasionally on a Show and Tell type day, Paul would bring a Tropical Snake or large Spider that the Picone's had discovered in the Fruit Crates delivered to their Store!

As for the Town's Delivery Trucks of that era, I remember the Herb Bowes Dry Cleaners Truck and the Brunella Bakery of course. Sometimes Herb Bowes would pay a penny a hanger returned which supplemented our allowances here and there

Chapter Fourteen

School Days

Back in the day, I recall Dundas having the reputation for having the best drinking water in the Hamilton area. Originally there was a reservoir on the road leading to the Golf Course which fed the Town's Water requirements. My Brother working for the Town in his late Teens once coated that basin with tar. I remember one of my Uncles driving for Tuckett's Tobacco of Hamilton would drop into our house for a drink of water when making Dundas deliveries.

I remember the first time he arrived stating to my Mother that he was stopping in to water his horse and went straight into the bathroom. Exciting at the prospect of seeing a Horse, I ran to the front door to look out. The Doors on the truck were closed and I went to my Mother in the kitchen asking for her largest bowl. She asked me why and I said to fill it with water for the horse. Upon leaving the Bathroom he took a heavy scolding from my Mother for an inappropriate remark. Which of course went over my head as they told me there was no horse, but I didn't believe them. I was convinced the Horse was out there and as we couldn't have a dog there was no way in hell she'd let a horse in the house!

On these visits, my Uncle would take a glass from the Kitchen Cupboard, have a drink of water, then rinse the glass putting it back in the cupboard!! Horrified, I would motion to my Mother who always silenced me with a wave of her hand. Once he left the glass would be retrieved and washed. Funny as if I did that it would have been a backhand not a wave.

In addition to the Dundas Water, was a concrete spring-fed Horse Trough, 3/4's of the way up the Hill past District High School. Most if not all of us Dundas Kids back in the day, while walking up the hill would have a drink of the water flowing from the pipe spilling into the trough. I remember Folks always stopping there, filling up 1-gallon glass bottles with the spring water! In later years, it had a warning sign placed there by Public Health warning that the water was unsafe to drink but people kept stopping. That trough and feeder pipe were later removed to prevent people from continuing that long-time practice.

I had always been interested in the fairer sex since the day I had brought the little Blonde Girl home at recess from Kindergarten. I really didn't have much experience with girls at that time. I mean, I had a sister but she being 14 years older than me was more of a Guardian (more on that later). I recall creating a love note one day in class probably around Grade 3. Not having a lot of time to create a Hallmark version it was pretty basic. "I love you, do you love me?" followed by two checkboxes, Yes or No.

To be honest, I do not recall who I sent it to. If you're reading this now and it was you, please contact me. I'd appreciate the memory. Unfortunately it was intercepted by the Teacher who I will simply recall as Ms. P. and she did have a bit of an edge to her. Strong knuckles, too, I recall from having my ears boxed numerous times. Anyway, note in hand she promptly read it aloud to the entire class. I died a thousand deaths of embarrassment.

St. Augustines School

Actually there were two Ms. P's at St. Augustine's, at least during my time there. The second one in a later grade taught us music. Well at the least made us suffer through her ear-splitting singing! "Do ye know John Peel at the break of day?" no but I knew the Beach Boys and "If You Should Go to Venice" not quite, Toronto was a more likely destination. She also took no pity on my ears! Thinking back I am sure we would have paid more attention had it been taught with songs from the Top 40!

Who could forget Valentine's Day? As I think of it now, it was a rather cruel event for some kids. I recall a large Cardboard Box with a slit in it covered with Sweet Hearts Paper in the classroom. Kids would deposit their cards there addressed to other kids. Boys to Girls and vice versa. I recall that we all stuffed those single, small, brightly printed cards in that box.

Though I always got my fair share of those "Be My Valentine Cards" back, a number of kids both boys and girls fared poorly in this veiled popularity contest. I can recall attempting to share some of my cards with a few boys but it really didn't make them feel any better. I have no idea if such practice continues in this day and age but surely if it does it would be structured so as to not be so egotistically devastating.

So here is a class photo of my Grade 4 Class at St. Augustine's School 1961.

When I pulled this photo out of an old scrapbook, I noticed that written on the back of it in my Mothers handwriting is Allan (On Cloud Nine). As you look at this photo it should be pretty easy to figure out where I am! (hint bottom left)

Grade 4 Class Photo

Actually it was a phrase I often heard so I must have spent a lot of time there. Here are some are some Teacher's comments on my report cards for a number of those years.

Mrs. Denomme – Grade 4 – "Conduct is not good! He annoys others around him"

Miss Golden – Grade 5 – "Good Worker but conduct is bad"

Mrs. Denomme – Grade 6 – "He could do better if he wasn't looking for a chance to cut up always"

Mr. Troy – Grade 7 – "Allan is a little excitable"

Mr. Troy – Grade 8 – "Allan's classroom habits show room for improvement" (likely from the Banana thrown at David Penney).

When I look at that Grade 4 Photo again as many of us would, it's a bit of a wistful memory and wonder of what happened to many of those kids. Certainly there are a handful of us still around in this area and I know of some now far away. Many I sincerely hope are well and still with us somewhere today while some others I know of are no longer here having passed away.

Jean Renton is in this photo, second row up from the bottom, third from the left. Newsworthy I am sure for us old Dundas Students, was that cursive writing, dropped from Ontario school curriculums years ago is being restored. Given it's long term absence there are younger folks out there today that can't even read it! In our day we were literally brow beat into learning it, writing and writing and with my iron grip on the pencil my hand often cramped.

Then to enhance our skills along came Fountain Pens and Ink Wells. Now about Jean Renton. She had two of the longest pigtails I had ever seen. She failed however to appreciate my innovative efforts at trying to dip the ends of them into my inkwell in the turquoise coloured ink! I had this idea to use them as an Artist Brush of sorts. When she told on me I guess it fell under "annoying others around him", at least according to Mrs. Denomme. Mrs. Denomme was an excellent Teacher but simply lacked in imagination. I have no idea where Jean may have ended up in her life but wherever she is I hope she is well!

DUNDAS SEPARATE SCHOOLS

JUNIOR AND INTERMEDIATE REPORT

GRADES 4, 5, 6, 7, 8

NAME Allan Duffin

GRADE 5   YEAR 1960 - 61

TEACHER Mrs. M. Denomme

MESSAGE FROM HIS EXCELLENCY

"Serious-minded parents realize that their responsibilities toward their children extend beyond mere physical care to the supervision of their intellectual and spiritual growth.

The school exists to help the parents to educate their children. Failure to provide religious training within the framework of this education means a lack of development in the noblest and the most vital of all spheres of activity, that of the spiritual life.

Religion must permeate every aspect of human endeavour, and is an essential part of true education.

The atmosphere of our homes must be thoroughly Catholic, inculcating in our children an intelligent and constant practice of our faith. Our schools must be imbued with this same spirit.

Education must embrace not only knowledge and the acquisition of skills for the pursuit of knowledge, but also the formation of character continuous attention to the deliberate practice of the Christian virtues.

Home, church, and school must be harmoniously blended like root, trunk, and branch, in the educational process."

✠ J. F. RYAN,
Bishop of Hamilton.

As for "Puppy Love" experiences, I certainly had my fair share and there is one young lady who I will never forget and will always be entwined with my memory of a famous historical event that happened one November day. Colleen Kennedy was perhaps not the most glamorous girl in our class but I did for a while have a secret crush on her.

On November 22nd, 1963 shortly after lunch, the Principal came on the intercom and her exact words were that "Mr. Kennedy has been shot and killed in Dallas". Everyone immediately turned, staring at poor Colleen who had turned a shade of white! Though my memory is not positive, I think that given President Kennedy was Catholic, we were allowed to go home then too.

Around Grade 8 likely as most Boys, I began to take a bit more notice of the fairer sex. The crushes now became much less secretive. Though St. Augustine's was a Catholic School, my female friendships were certainly not limited to girls from there. I recall walking down Melville Street one Saturday holding hands with a young lady from Central Public. Along came a large blue Ford Sedan, cruising slowly by us with the Driver eyeing us with the zeal of a Police Officer. It was however a Priest, our Church Pastor, Monsignor K. I recall being extremely uncomfortable under this intense observation and angry to boot returning his glare.

Monday morning at School, I was called down to the Principal's Office now a somewhat regular occurrence. It was another Nun then and I don't recall her name but she asked me to run an errand for her. Handing me a small box of Church Donation Envelopes, she asked me to take them down to the Monsignor's Office at the Rectory, the Priests living quarters beside the Church. I immediately saw thru the ruse but had little choice so away I went.

He closed the door to his office and then mentioned he had seen me with this girl and he knew she didn't go to our School. I then got lectured on the trouble I could get into. It was borderline traumatic for me but I had to sit through it and then returned to school. Knowing I was Fatherless at the time, perhaps he felt duty-bound to look out for me. In any case, I don't think he said anything to my Mother as it was never mentioned. Funny thing though it was Colleen Garry who was the first Girl I ever kissed and was a devout Catholic Girl!

My older Brother Billy had been an Altar Boy at St. Augustine's and I had just started training to follow suit. My Mother thru Social Assistance had got me a Membership at the Hamilton YMCA, where I was able to go and play sports and swim etc. Shortly thereafter Monsignor K called me in after I had missed an altar Boy practice session as I'd been at the Y. Upon hearing where I was, I recall his stern warning that I would have to make a choice in that I could not be an Altar Boy and continue going to the YMCA. I remember telling him clearly that he'd have to find another Altar Boy and I left.

Things back then were pretty strict with the Catholic Church. On Religious Feast (Holiday) Days we got the day off school but you were expected to be in Church on those mornings. Our Teachers kept a tally and if you were not seen in church, you'd hear about it the next school day. My Brother had taken the Bus to Hamilton for High School at the Catholic Cathedral Boys. I rebelled at this continued religious strictness and the coming separation from many of my friends. My Mother finally relented allowing me to attend Parkside for High School, only a block or so farther than St. Augustine's School from our House.

St. Augustine's Church

As for the Monsignor, I did even the playing field a number of years later. Then working as an Orderly in the Henderson General Hospital's Emergency Department in Hamilton, I saw an Advertisement in the Hamilton Spectator. It was for the position of Ambulance Attendant in Burlington. Imagining the action and adventure of that occupation I applied. As it turned out, the Owner of the Ambulance Service was a member of a Pentecostal Church. At the end of my interview, he advised he would hire me but required a letter from my Minister or Priest indicating I was of good moral character.

While I was basically, it had been quite a while since I had attended Church though still living literally across the Street from St. Augustine's. I needed a plan and after careful thought, came up with one. I discovered the Monsignor was still at St. Augustine's which initially dashed my hopes given my previous experiences with him. Hmm, he obviously was much older now. Would he remember me? Considering my circumstances he was my only option.

The Henderson Hospital, now Juravanski is on Concession Street in Hamilton. Not very far away there was another Catholic Church, and upon doing some checking I learned the Pastor's Name there and the times for their Services. Gripping the phone somewhat, I called the St. Augustine's Rectory mentioning my name and requirements. I held my breath as silence followed. "Hello Allan it is nice to hear from you, please come over for a chat". With due trepidation, I went over and he sat behind a desk studying me, much the same as he had many years ago.

It didn't take long for the obvious statement to be made, " I don't recall seeing you at Church for many years". I explained my place of work mentioning that I worked a lot of Night Shifts. I went on to explain that on Sundays I had Breakfast at a Restaurant near the Hospital and then attended Mass at the other Church mentioning their Priest's name. Okay well at least some of my explanation was the truth and the balance was after all only a bit of a white lie but it sufficed in getting my Letter of Reference and as they say, "The rest is History".

Chapter Fifteen

Old Time Deliveries

Driving along one day, I passed one of the few remaining Becker's Milk Stores and recalled when they were introduced around here. As bread and milk stores, they effectively sounded the death knell of the door-to-door milk and bread deliveries of my childhood. Thinking back, at our front door we received Bread, Milk, and Ice for the Icebox and even coal for our stoves. The Coal Yards where the coal was stored at that time in Dundas were located on Hatt Street behind the Post Office, where a Car Wash was located later and is today a modern facility housing an Eye Clinic.

The Coal Delivery Man used to scare me as he was covered head to toe in black soot with only the whites of his eyes showing. With his little Cap on he would carry the coal in a burlap sack over his shoulders. He'd come in the house and march back and forth down the Hallway and thru the Kitchen to the Bin out our back door. My Mother ordered Coal for our Stoves, and paid $17 a ton. In the winter, every morning it was my chore to fill two one-gallon coal pails for each stove.

I am sure horse and wagon deliveries had basically ceased in Dundas by the mid 50's. The one delivery truck though easily remembered was the milk truck which you could hear long before it came into view. It had a unique sound created by the rattle of the glass milk bottles in the wire containers. I can close my eyes and still hear it. That sound was perhaps amplified by the open doors on the truck given the frequent stops for either side of the street. The Valley City and Mountain View Dairies delivered their products throughout Dundas.

For our family it was the Valley City Dairy and their Guernsey Gold Milk with the 2-inch layer of cream at the top. My Mother used to turn the bottle upside down to mix in the cream. The Bottles had a cardboard disc-like top. Milk is noted of course for the development of strong bones. Given my physical adventures over the years without breaking a bone, that Guernsey Gold must have been good stuff!

Later on as I grew older, I learned a valuable lesson from my older Brother Billy. The practice of the day back then was to leave your empty milk bottles by your front door. You'd leave money and a note in the bottle for the milkman. He would come along early in the morning and gather them, leaving whatever your order was by the door.

I learned that if you needed to top up your allowance, you could visit a few Houses in the neighborhood. I can remember practicing how to get the money, mostly coins, out of the bottle without making noise! Now I know what you're thinking but hey, we never hit the same house more than once a month!! The Dairy though eventually caught on, likely hearing from some irate customers and issued tickets or tokens which ended that caper!

Who could forget the breadman!! There'd be a knock at the front door which this small boy would open and be at eye level with this huge wire basket. Though likely a marketing ploy by Jackson's Bakery back in the day, that basket would always seem to be bulging at the front with Chocolate Jelly Rolls, Donuts and Cakes. I'd stand there wide-eyed and drooling but before I could reach out the illusion was shattered by this stern voice in the background: "Just a Loaf of Bread please".

Jackson's Bakery was located in a large facility on Lemming Street in Hamilton and my friend Mike Roach's Father worked there. One Easter weekend when we were maybe 13 or 14, he got us a job at the Bakery on a Good Friday. We went there at midnight and worked on a Hot Cross Bun Assembly line fighting to keep awake all night long. There were a couple of different stations. The buns would come along on a conveyor in sections of 6.

There was a wooden bucket of sticky stuff with a wide paintbrush and you'd brush this glaze over the top of them. I remember seeing dead flies on the sides of the bucket that had drowned in it. As the night went on, so did the glaze, on my hands, face, hair and clothes. So we'd switch around but the next station was even worse! As the Buns came along the conveyor, these flat boxes had to be sprung open quickly and I remember getting small cuts on my gloveless hands. As you couldn't leave your position before a break, I'd just continually wipe my hands on my pants. You'd plop in 6 buns then a sheet of waxed paper and 6 more on the top. Yep, sticky and slippery buns and coming fast, like something out of an old I Love Lucy Episode!

So as you might imagine, occasionally some buns would somehow end up on the floor. There wasn't much grease or dirt down there that couldn't be easily wiped off as you brushed them across your pants when no one was looking. We quickly learned to hide those that didn't look perfect on the bottom of the package covered with a sheet of waxed paper. Then Buns on the top then on to be wrapped in cellophane and then be stacked ready for delivery. If anyone ever did notice an inferior product, it was never brought to the attention of the two one-night special employees! As my Mother always used to say, "You have to eat a pound of dirt before you die" anyway" so it was all good!

Before we knew it, dawn had arrived and we were finished, likely sound asleep in the back of the car after a couple of blocks but rich!!! As I look back now, I think it was about 5 years before I could eat or even look at a Hot Cross Bun again.

Last but not least, how about the Guy we called "The Yummy Man"!! And a version thereof is still around today, you'd hear this truck long before it appeared playing Turkey in the Straw Music and the Kids would go running! Not to the Truck but home to ask for money. If my Mother had some change and I wasn't in the dog house for something, I could score some Ice Cream or a Popsicle and it was cheap, whereas today, I kiss a 20-dollar bill goodbye when buying a few kids a treat.

Chapter Sixteen

The Bus

The Dundas of my childhood had two Buses that travelled thru town. The local Hamilton Street Railway (HSR) "Dundas" Bus which went back and forth to Hamilton and the Grey Coach lines Bus.

The Grey Coach Bus was an important link for Folks living just outside of town in the Grand Vista Survey at the top of the hill or Greensville. It passed those locations and carried on up Hwy# 8 towards Kitchener. Many of the kids simply walked up the hill and home most days from School. Greensville was a small village-like place but also the location of Tip Top Canners, a post office/general store and Fenton's Variety.

One of my earliest memories of buses in Dundas was watching them go in and out of the Bus Garage which was originally the Dundas Curling Rink and today of course, the Shawn and Ed Brewery beside Memorial Square. I recall my first Bus Ride into Hamilton travelling with my Mother. As we didn't have a car, this was a major adventure for me. I liked the diesel smell and sat by the window with my nose pressed against the glass. She took that bus ride faithfully every month to pay the mortgage on our house in person at the Catholic Credit Union in Hamilton. Then we'd go shopping in a number of stores downtown.

My absolute favorite was the old Eaton's' Store with its scary elevators that travelled quickly leaving your stomach at the starting location and skillfully operated by white-gloved operators. As it quickly rushed up or down, you could see the building bricks go by through the glass-walled elevator. Eaton's always had incredible window displays too especially at Christmas with animated figures. At Easter time we'd watch baby chicks hatching thru the Store's Front window and although fascinating to watch it did dampen my enthusiasm for eggs for a couple of months.

Then bundled up with shopping bags we'd stand outside Mills China Shop on King Street to catch the Bus home. As I got older of course my friends and I would often go to Hamilton on the Bus. I remember when I started working during summers in Hamilton; I'd catch the Bus by Glessnings Coffee Shop beside the original Dundas Library now the Carnegie Gallery.

One summer, I was smitten by a young lady who got on the Bus with me every morning though I never had the nerve to strike up a conversation. I don't remember where she got off either but I should have been braver. A number of years later our Dundas Superstar Ian Thomas composed "Right Before Your Eyes," a song that captured my memory of those brief bus encounters perfectly.

I worked summer relief for a few years in what is now known as the Juravinski Hospital in Hamilton as a Porter walking miles each day delivering lab specimens and wheeling patients about. By the end of my shift, I was tired out completely and the Bus journey back to Dundas was always an adventure. I would first have to catch a bus in front of the Hospital to take me downtown to catch the Dundas Bus. Though the Mills China shop location in Hamilton was popular, if you wanted a seat it was better to go to the old Bus Terminal first.

I am sure many folks will remember the muffled announcements at old-time Bus Stations. "Dundas Bus mfmmmmmmning on Platform 9." When it rolled up to the China Shop on King Street, on climbed all of the ladies like my Mother who'd been shopping. Along with their shopping bags and various other packages, seating was always limited and standing for the entire trip back to town was often necessary. One Day our Bus hit a skunk just before the University Plaza. With our eyes and noses burning most of us got off there and walked the rest of the way home.

One of Dundas's great enterprises back in the day was the Brunella Bakery. For a number of us, those memories are tied to Fernando and Adele Citrigno who we went to school with. Their parents established and operated the Bakery. As I began to write this, I wondered when it actually did open and after some research I discovered that the Brunella Bakery is referenced in a Statistics Canada Report as being a new Business at 115 King St. West in Dundas in December of 1962. It grew to become a very popular Dundas Bakery and was renowned for the quality of its Italian Breads and Specialties.

Fernando (Ferny) was a good friend of mine who I grew up with right thru our teenage years. Adele, Fernando's Sister was popular with the Girls too and I enjoyed harassing her with her Brother as young boys want to do! The Bakery was a well-known busy place and also provided Delivery Service. They operated a Red GM Panel Truck with the name painted in a gold leaf style on each side. While I could not locate a photo of their actual truck, here is an example.

Truck similar to Brunella Bakery, Dundas, Ont

As Ferny and Adele grew older, they also worked in the Family Business.

Once Ferny acquired his Driver's License, he began to make the deliveries. Though Brunella was a Dundas Bakery, I was quite surprised to learn of their loyal Customer Base that ranged well into Hamilton's Italian Neighborhoods. Considering the number of Italian Bakeries in Hamilton, they obviously faired very well with the competition! Occasionally I'd go with Ferny to help him out on their delivery route. We'd drive along and conduct numerous home deliveries where I would jump out get the item and place it between the front doors of the Houses.

Thinking back it's funny what you remember, we'd deliver a lot of the round Italian-style Calabrese Breads in their paper bags and other products. You had to be careful with those paper bags too and I recall a few loaves bouncing off the sidewalks as the bag ripped open. In a few delivery stops, the housewives would start speaking in Italian to me which I didn't understand of course. Ferny would say, "Ignore them, we don't have time to socialize or for you to learn Italian anyway". After seeing one of those "loaf bounces", one lady ran screaming at me in Italian and literally chased me back to the truck! Ferny simply commented "Don't worry about it," and calmly drove away. On the odd time, I might score a free loaf of Calabrese if we had any leftovers!

While David Leigh would garner his Star on the Dundas Walk of Fame at a later time with his "Beach Balls" Pizza, Brunella to my recollection offered the 1st Pizzas in Dundas. For a period of time, Brunella in addition to their main location, also opened a Pizza Shop on the Southside of King Street just down from the Jaggard's Store, across the Street from the Melbourne Hotel. So Ferny, obviously being taught by his Mom and Dad, worked that location in the evenings making Pizzas and of course, "the Gang" would hang out to keep him company! Then as you might imagine, Ferny would treat us with free Pizza Slices and often get into trouble with his Father!

To this day, while I don't actually remember how long the Pizza Shop location was open, it certainly was not for a long period of time and only Ferny would know if it was the "Free Pizza" that eventually did it. In my later Teens, I lost contact with Ferny once I started working outside of Dundas and the last I had heard was that he was selling Fiat Cars somewhere. Sampling the Brunella Bakery Bread was my first experience with Calabrese Bread and it remains my favorite still today after all these years!

As they say, "truth is stranger than fiction". In the last few years, as I began to assemble this book, I searched unsuccessfully for my old Friend Fernando, and then suddenly thru an online social app, we discovered each other. It was remarkable as it had been over 55 years and here we were, neighbors living merely a few streets from each other.

So here is the rest of the Brunella Story. In 1972, Fernando was roused from his sleep by a telephone call advising him their Bakery was on fire. He rose quickly and his Father asked who was calling. Not wishing to upset him, Ferny mentioned there was a fire near the Bakery and left for it. As he drove in the Driveway, numerous Fire Trucks blocked it and there was his Father directly behind him. His

Father rushed forward taking a Fire Axe from a Firefighter and broke down the front door rescuing their Dog Hobo who fortunately survived. While there had been some Family discussion about the Kids taking over the Bakery, Fernando's Father felt Fernando and Adele would be better off pursuing other ventures and later sold the business.

Fernando went on to a successful career in Sales Training spanning much of Canada and the USA. As for Adele, it was Dundas's loss and North Bay's gain as she spent most of her married life there. She operated a number of successful businesses being very well known in the community. She was President of the Ladies Auxiliary of the Prestigious Italian Davidi Club for a number of years. She also was the driving force thru unsettled waters in establishing North Bay's Nippissing Serenity Hospice. Sadly for her family and the Community, it was an incredible loss when she passed away relatively early in life a few years ago.

I'll finish this chapter with a story about my older Brother Billy who I will remind you is 6 years or so older than me and note a number of his friends back in old Dundas.

Walter (Tex) Rogerson, Frank (Busty) Fama, Danny, Pat and Paul Penney, (I grew up with David), Jerome Duckworth, Bill McGinley, Bill Grisdale, David Hewer, Dougie Wong and many others. Back in that era, Jerome Duckworth was a well-known and loved free spirit and a common companion to many of the boys in the day. He was for a long time one of my Brother's best Friends. One time, the downstairs apartment in our House was vacant and my Brother and Jerome were helping my Mother repaint it. Being later in the afternoon on a Friday, they stopped as we were getting ready to leave for a weekend at the Cottage.

As the painting was almost finished, Jerome offered to complete it which my Mother graciously agreed to. We returned from the Cottage late on a Sunday Night. The next morning, my Mother went downstairs to have a look. At first she was dazzled by the gleaming white picket fence separating our property from the next-door neighbors that had been freshly painted. The Interior Walls as left were finished perfectly however as well; Jerome had decided to paint the Bathtub, Sink and faucets with some white paint as well to give them a "fresh look"! My Mother said nothing, paid him and later cleaned off the paint. Jerome displayed great creativity while wielding a paintbrush and perhaps had missed his "True Calling".

Many many years later at a Central Hamilton Tim Horton's Drive Thru, I saw Jerome cleaning an adjacent Variety Store Parking Lot. Being in a Drive Thru Line, I never had the chance to engage him in a conversation though I wonder if he would have remembered an old friend's kid Brother. I understand that in his later years, Jerome was a St. Joseph's Villa Resident in Dundas and passed away a few years ago.

Chapter Seventeen

The Dances

Check your source of Music and listen again to "Let's Dance" by Chris Montez which was released in 1962. When I hear the pounding of those drums again, it rockets me back to "Teen Town" and my discovery that Girls could be a whole lot more than annoying. Teen Town as some of my vintage will recall was upstairs in the Old Dundas Town Hall. My older Sister Carole had encouraged me to go through the thought of dancing with a girl and in front of other people was a bit frightening! To this day, the memory persists that I wasn't as cool as some of my Dance Floor competitors there in attracting the fairer sex. Likely to keep haircut costs down, in those sometimes awkward adolescent times, I was sent to Bill O'Reilly's Barbershop at the front of the Melbourne Hotel for a Brush Cut. I think Bill was one of the original Dundas Barbers of my younger days before Felix another well-known Dundas Barber came along.

I'd stand in front of the mirror getting ready for Teen Town, furiously brushing that 1 inch of hair left hoping it would somehow grow longer. Then, dressing as spiffily as possible, off I went with nervous excitement and a dollop of trepidation. In the end, most of the time that preparation was in vain for this classic Wallflower as I sat there lacking the required courage for the dance floor. While my introduction to Girls en masse had been at school, annoying them had been my sport of the day. This Teen Town place though was often full of them and many were new to me including a number of real "Lookers" from other schools. The fact that we boys had suddenly become of interest to them too was exciting! Maybe my older Sister was on to something here. Most of my experiences there however were of borderline fantasy to a large degree given my uber shyness.

My curiosity about it all though remained aroused and it struck me that if you were the Disc Jockey that could offer a significant edge.

So I sat and watched them dance listening to Gene Pitney's "Only Love Can Break a Heart" while building up what little nerve I had to ask someone to dance. Looking back as us Guys would say, I got "Shot Down" often and the first time a Girl said yes, I almost passed out!!

What I eventually learned though would be of great value at Shade Blue Dance Nights a number of years later. At Teen Town, though I have long forgotten the few girls that I awkwardly shuffled with on rare occasions to those teenage anthems. The Bad Boys were there too even at that early age with stashed mickies in the washroom. I learned about cigarettes and other things outside too like getting beat up a few times for being shy and nerdy I suppose but I survived.

Later at Parkside High School, there were Dances and sometimes "Sadie Hawkins" nights where the Girls got to ask the boys to dance. There, older now, I managed to get my share of dances with different girls. This resulted in a significant confidence boost just in time for "Shade Blue' a Friday Night Club established in the Club Safari, the old Roxy Theatre for the younger set. This was the "big time" now with live Bands like Bobby Washington and the Soul Society, and others. One of my old friends then in our dual pursuits of the fairer sex was Fernando Citrigno the Bakery Boy and we'd go to Shade Blue often together.

Now there was a guy with great hair which I was always jealous of. If you're reading this now Ferny, sorry but I just have to share this. So I'd go over to his place, an apartment upstairs beside the old Music Hall and I'd be antsy to get going. But for Ferny, this was a big deal and he had to look perfect!! So there he's standing in front of the bathroom mirror forever with a hair net on patting every curl into place. We'd also share some of his Mom or Sister Adele's tan makeup which we touched up our Zits with!

The Bonus of Shade Blue was that you could really play the field there. There was never a short supply of young ladies and often imports from Hamilton too!! Once you connected with a cool girl, you could dance the night away though often just like Cinderella's they'd disappear at the "witching hour" and be spirited away. Not in Gold Carriages either, just "Fathers Cars". Now being good boys, we wouldn't dare let those fair Damsels remaining walk home alone on the dangerous streets of Dundas! But I do recall a very safe pathway on Moonlit Nights along the Spencer Creek thru the Woods behind the McMaster Pottery, just saying!

Now mentioning Shade Blue a bit later, I was with my then-steady girlfriend Kathy Smith and her friend Heidi Sattler and her steady Bruce Picken. At some point, a Donnybrook of sorts started which we were not involved in though an errant fist found its way to my face dropping me. Bruce stepped into the melee which eventually stopped and we regrouped outside. We survived and to this day, my slightly indented lower front tooth is a reminder of it every time I look in a mirror.

I also spent a number of nights at Shade Blue with Judy Whatmough of Greensville and despite her Father Howard always driving her home at the end of the night, she became my Wife a few years later!

After enduring Brush Cuts for my tween-like years, I only had the luxury of enjoying Beatle-like locks for a scant few years after. My hair quickly started to recede in my early 20's which was most unfair. While I did have a long EMS Career, I did realize that long ago Teen Town fantasy when I started a side business as a Disc Jockey that was quite successful for over 20 years. This was also a very good outlet for me over that time as it was a totally different line of work from my EMS Career.

Before I leave the Disc Jockey experience, I have to share this Story. I didn't just play music at some area events. Some evenings, I would do a take-off on let's make a deal. I would have 3 or 4 boxes gift-wrapped sitting on a table with the bottoms open. 3 would be covering gag prizes and 1 with a nice prize as supplied by the organization I was playing for. Some nights I'd also give the winner a choice of an Envelope in my pocket too that might have money or a couple of aspirins. The Contestants would be Door Prizes or Spot Dance Winners.

One afternoon as I was setting up equipment in an area Hall, I got an idea when I noticed a storage room door near my setup. I called a buddy of mine who was renting a Farmhouse in West Flamboro and asked him if he could get me a live chicken. An hour later, there it was in an old milk crate and I stashed it inside this closet-like storage room just off what would be the Dance Floor.

Allan the Disc Jockey

A Spot Dance winner later was given a choice about one of the gift-wrapped boxes on a table, my left suit pocket or Door Number 1 which of course was where the chicken was. As luck would have it, they chose the Door. What I didn't realize was that the chicken had gotten out of the box. When I opened the door, it rushed out loudly squawking into the Dance Floor area surrounded by 150 people. It was absolutely insane and brought the house down. Though the gag worked beyond my wildest expectations, the worst was yet to come.

It was a Valentine's Dance and the winner declined to take the prize. So here it was later at 2 a.m., wind howling minus 10 temperature and I am stuck with a live chicken. So I managed to get it back into the Milk Crate and took it home, not having the heart to wring its neck. When I got home, I realized that if I put it in the garage it might die from the extremely low temperature. I couldn't bring it to the house because I had two Cats. What to do? We lived in a townhouse at the time with a Bathroom just inside the front door. So I took the chicken into the Bathroom having put it in a milk crate and stacked some LPs on the top to hold it in.

So after securing the chicken in the downstairs bathroom, I went to bed. A number of hours later being dimly awake, I heard my wife who was a Sunday School Teacher at the time conversing downstairs with an elderly neighbor lady who normally accompanied her to church.

On nights when I was out playing music I got off the hook and didn't have to go. I remember thinking, gee I hope she doesn't have to use the bathroom. My friend the chicken unbeknownst to me had again escaped the crate. Sure enough she went to use the bathroom and it was pandemonium. Squawking, screaming and what I knew was my wife stomping up the stairs! I lay there pretending to sleep and suddenly heard this seething whispering voice of my wife in my ear, " I don't care how it got there but if you want to continue living here, get it out of the living room NOW!"

Gee, some people just have no sense of humour. Now if you're wondering about the chicken, it ended up on a neighbor's dinner table a few days later.

Chapter Eighteen

The Show

Growing up as Kids, when we went out to the Movie Theatre, we called it "The Show". In Dundas our Theatre depending on your vintage was known as the Majestic (1929-48), Roxy (1948-61) and for a brief time later, upstairs in the Old Music Hall. There were in earlier times a few other locations in Dundas where films were shown like the Wonderland Theatre here around the turn of the Century.

Early Dundas Theatre, Dundas Museum and Archives

For most of us though the traditional location at 24 King St. West, housed the Theatre we knew as ours. Today of course that tanned brick building still stands housing the Horn of Plenty and now having Apartments in the ample space above the original structure. For you nostalgia buffs, the original downstairs washroom remained unchanged from the theatre days when I checked it out a few years ago.

My first experience at the Roxy which I do not recall was often recited by my older Sister Carole, the "Duffin Clan Elder" responsible for maintaining Family Lore. She took me to see Disney's Snow White and the 7 Dwarfs and took great delight over the years repeatedly embarrassing me over how badly frightened I was by the Witch!

On Saturdays, it was a classic Institution for Dundas Kids attending afternoon matinees. Depending on the main feature, Kids might dress as Cowboys and bring their often confiscated cap guns. I remember the Fastest Draw Contest. Sometimes also there would be other mini-talent contests and/or prize draws. It was something I'd looked forward to all week though I occasionally miss out due to my numerous "groundings".

I loved the freedom, going there with friends on a Saturday Afternoon. It was great fun and after devouring our Popcorn we'd flatten the boxes and zing them through the air. When we weren't making kingers with the chestnuts in the fall, we'd often let them fly bouncing off the Screen. The individual charged with overseeing this excited melee was the venerable "Mrs. Spratt" who patrolled the aisles, flashlight glaring with the demeanor of a Drill Sergeant! Often we'd be watching where she was instead of whatever was on the Screen. If you threw something you had to slouch down quickly as not to be noticed.

Invariably though there were a few of us Matinee attendees who occasionally were ejected and came home early, then you'd have to come up with an excuse and complain about the short movie! Funny what sticks in your mind, but in the back row on the right side as you entered the seating area, there was always a Man sitting just on the right-hand end seat at the back of the middle row. I don't remember him ever bothering anyone nor am I suggesting he did. It was just unusual that he was always the only Adult attendee alone there on very noisy Saturday afternoons.

I remember my first two "Grownup" films that I saw there with my Mother and have never forgotten. The "10 Commandments" which scared me into paying more attention at Church at least for a few Sundays and a few years later, Rogers and Hammerstein's "South Pacific" where I fell in love with Mitzi Gaynor. In 1960 at 11 years old, my friend Graeme McMaster and I went to the Roxy one Saturday Night to see William Castle's "13 Ghosts". On entry, you were given cardboard framed glasses to wear. The plastic lenses were red on one side and blue on the other. When the ghosts appeared if you were too scared to look, you'd view thru the blue lens or red if you were brave!

Margaret Hamilton, the Witch of Wizard of Oz fame played the Creepy Housekeeper. Check out this link here for the original Trailer which you can find on YouTube. It will set up the scene that follows here perfectly. https://youtu.be/Ocdb4qI2PqE As I now listen to the Announcer on this trailer, it strikes me that it is likely Paul Frees, a famous voice actor whose fame includes the welcoming voice to Disney's Haunted Mansion!

As I recall, Graeme and I after the film, were outwardly full of bravado though for us at the time it was a scary movie. We left the Roxy and went to Graeme's house where no one was supposed to be home. The House was in darkness from the outside. We went in and went upstairs heading for his bedroom. Down the hall the bathroom light was on and suddenly out stepped what we saw as the silhouette of a Man! Instinctively we both hit the floor covering our heads and screaming. Though I am not sure who got the Lion's share of the fright, fortunately for us it was Graeme's older Brother Malcolm who was not expected to be home.

The Roxy closed a year or so later. Thereafter, I remember seeing Disney's Davey Crockett upstairs at the Music Hall sitting on Card Table like chairs. Unfortunately Matinee films were only shown there for a brief period of time. Dundas's Music Hall was later condemned with what was declared an unsafe floor. It was closed, literally moth balled for a number of years. Of course, we managed to get in there during that time for some urban like exploring. I once found a Theatre Lobby Card behind the stage for the 1956 Film Trapeze starring Burt Lancaster and Tony Curtis

Now going to the show meant taking the Bus into Hamilton. One Christmas my friend Norman scored a Book of Famous Player Theatre Tickets from Santa. We bused into Hamilton on Boxing Day to see Disney's "Babes in Toyland" at the Tivoli in 1961. Back then, Boxing Day was a very popular day to go to the Show. For many years I recall standing in huge lines freezing waiting to buy tickets at different Theatre Box Offices.

When we arrived at the Tivoli, there was a huge lineup but as we didn't have to buy tickets with his Gift Book, they let us in right away! Awesome! Having our pick of seats we chose of course, front row center. The Film impressed us so much that when it ended, we came out and used more tickets to get right back in and see it again!!

A further note on the Roxy Theatre's History, Eph Slote purchased the Theatre in 1961 and its days as a Theatre ended soon thereafter. A Hardwood Dance Floor was put in for dancing over the top of many of the original Theatre seats which slanted down towards the screen. It became the Club Safari Dance Hall and was popular for a number of years including Friday Nights for Shade Blue as previously noted. Many years later, the original seats under the floor were declared a fire hazard. They were removed and sold to the Port Dover Little Theatre.

Chapter Nineteen

Fun and Games

A few weeks ago, at a yard sale, I happened to see an old Lido Toy Bowling Game with large plastic 10 Pins. What a flash that gave me of a rather unusual game we used to play at my Friend Norman's house, when no one was home of course. Bowling to us was just plain boring and once again we fired up our imaginations!

That Dundas House, Park and Sydenham, at that time had two Bathrooms upstairs. At the top of the stairs was the smaller of the two with the Toilet. Then over to the left side of the landing up there was the larger room with the Tub. We would open the Toilet Bathroom Door and raise the Toilet Seat. Then we'd stand at the bottom of the stairs and take turns throwing the Bowling Pins up into the bathroom and you got a point for every Pin that landed in the Toilet. As I write this, yes it might appear strange but at 9-10 years old it was great fun! Unfortunately, though the game was unique, we never got to play it for very long.

The first downside was the questions from his parents about where the mysterious marks on the walls came from, which of course no one knew! In retrospect, it was a miracle that we never broke the window. What ended the practice was when we forgot to take a Pin out of the toilet one day! Norman disappeared the following weekend and I held my breath hoping there would be no phone call. Our Mothers were not friends per se but they knew and often acknowledged each other in the IGA Grocery Store Aisle. However when they were on the Telephone together it was an exchange of vital intelligence often damaging our best laid plans.

As my Mother was not an Animal Lover, I never had pets for longer than a few days save for Toby the Budgie as previously noted. In addition to my frozen Hamster, we also had a Dog but for only a week or so. Too much noise and mess we were told. We also had a Raccoon briefly that my Brother got somewhere and it was caged in the backyard. I felt sorry for it and let it out. Speaking of Raccoons, a man used to walk down our street with one on a leash!

Norman had a Bassett Hound named Checkers that we used to take for walks sometimes. Checkers was a low rider being so fat his belly barely clearing the sidewalk. He enjoyed his food and I think had his share of table scraps too! He eventually had a Heart Attack and keeled over. It was a solemn occasion when I attended his funeral in their back garden where a rose bush was planted over him later.

At a younger age, I recall being at Gerry Ausseum's House which was 2-3 doors up York Road from the Cemetery Gates. Living on Melville Street, it was much shorter to walk home thru the Cemetery than go the long way around down to Park St and across.

One night in the winter, I stayed there later in the afternoon and it got dark outside.

I mentioned my nervousness about having to walk thru the Cemetery but if I took the long way around, I would be late for Dinner. We went downstairs to his Dad's workshop and took a baby food jar, filled it with some finishing nails and boiled hot water in a kettle and put the jar in a bag. I took it with me ready to swing it at anything that might jump out at me in the Cemetery. Fortunately I didn't encounter anyone but it was terrifying walking thru there in the dark.

In the Summer, Norman and I often went fishing and in the days when we didn't feel like walking to the Marsh we would go down to the Spencer Creek under the Ogilvie Street Bridge where the Metro Store now stands. Suckers, Shiners and Chub were always in abundance there. There was one huge Chub we called Sammy which between the two of us we had on the line a few times but he was a smart old fish and always managed to get off.

I remember we would sometimes take a couple of slices of luncheon meat for bait when our worms were in short supply.

Sometimes if we had a Sucker or two, we'd throw them through the open windows of Bertram's on Ogilvie Street and run like hell!

When we did decide to take the extended hike to the Marsh (Cootes Paradise), Norman's Mother would make us Cornmeal Balls which we would use for bait to catch Carp. One day on a Saturday, we sold a 5-6 lb Carp to a Man in a fancy Suit who had walked down there after attending a Religious Service on a Saturday for 5 bucks a fortune!

We often went Worm Picking on area lawns and I remember being chased off a Chiropractors Lawn at Park and Sydenham Road. Some people didn't like worms being picked on their lawns. We christened him the Worm Hog!

As small-town routines go, there was an elderly Lady who walked the streets of our neighborhood dressed in black with a black Pill Box Hat, wire spectacles and a matching veil over her face. One night we got this great idea to pick worms in the Grove Cemetery where nobody would chase us out. It was dark of course and we had our headband flashlights. Hearing a noise, we looked up and there was the old lady dressed in black. I think the can of worms must have gone 20 feet up in the air as we ran for our lives.

Church was always an interesting and sometimes fun experience, especially if two or three of us kids sat together. At the quietest part of the service, someone would fart and we'd start to snicker and elsewhere some older folks would even laugh. While Church was certainly not our favorite place to go, At St Augustine's the Lawn on the Melville Street Side was a great open space to play. The concrete support wall at the back of the Church facing the Central Public School often substituted for the Alamo being attacked from the playground there.

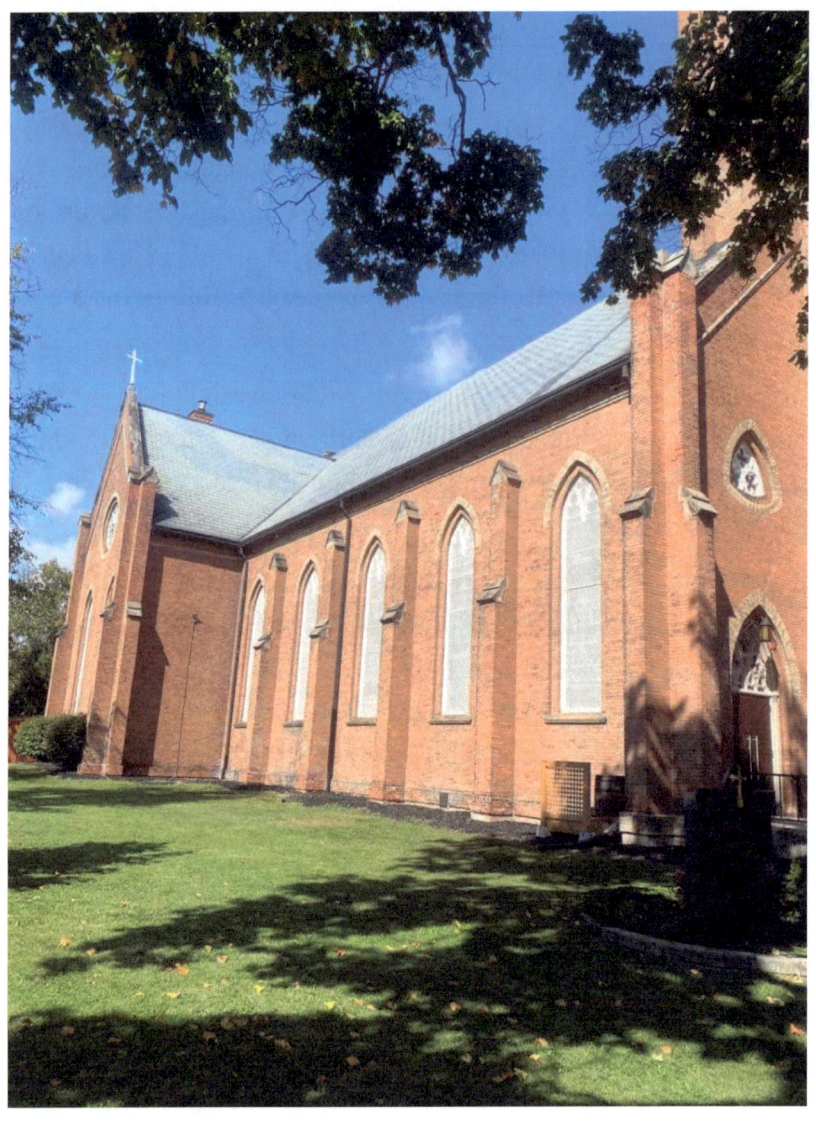

    Another fun pursuit during our Robin Hood Phase was firing the blunt end arrows straight up in the air from our fiber glass bows and then running with your hands covering your head, amazing what fun, bored kids could come up with.

    Another great pastime was throwing or kicking a football up onto the angled Church Roof, then running along waiting for it to drop to try and catch it. It made for a great Fall Saturday afternoon until the Priests chased us off the property. Yes the Church did have fancy stained glass windows, but they were covered with a heavy screened mesh. When the Priests suddenly appeared I don't know why we ran, they knew who we were and living so close they simply walked over to my House and ratted us out! "But Mom I wasn't over at the Church today," I cried while being sentenced to another incarceration. My excuse of a number of other kids out there who looked like me, never worked no matter how sincere my explanation was.

Chapter Twenty

BAD BOYS

Looking back, my first time as a Bad Boy happened after being influenced by a neighborhood Kid at around the tender age of 12 or so years old. He fascinated me when he showed me all of his various treasures hidden away in a secret place in his backyard. The most incredible thing too was that he hadn't spent any money to acquire these things! He went on to explain how you could take things for free from a store as long as you moved quickly when no one was watching!

As a young, Oliver Twist-like pupil, I listened attentively and thought this was the greatest secret I had ever learned! He went on to explain that you should be careful what you brought home too as it might raise questions from your parents! This was of course in my pre-working days and my meager allowance never seemed to last very long.

So there I was on a rainy Saturday afternoon, alone at the Circular Comic Rack in O'Neil's Variety. Annie O'Neal sat at the counter and I think was on the phone with someone. Quickly and carefully I folded a comic book and slipped it into my coat. Casually, I continued to check out various comics and finally decided it was time to make my getaway! I turned and started for the door and there she stood blocking my way with her arms folded with these dark, piercing eyes boring a hole through me! In a very low voice came the command, "Open your coat"! Now, absolutely petrified, I opened my coat and the comic dropped to the floor!! Pointing to the back of the store, "That way" she intones and I slowly shuffle back there.

She sat me down and started the discussion, my name and where I lived. I can still hear her, "Oh, Duffin, I know Mrs. Duffin". I sank lower in the chair, my fate sealed now! She sat there and gave me a lecture I remember to this day about stealing and how it hurt her livelihood and how I could end up in Reform School. So I say, "but I am already in school at St. Augustine's". "You won't be any longer, Reform School is a prison for bad children!"

I sat there wide-eyed and terrified while she pondered who to call first, the Police or my Mother! I think at that point, I would have preferred she call the Police!! Anyway after what seemed like an eternity she decided not to call the Police or even my Mother!! I did though solemnly have to swear to never steal again and that I was also to never come in her Store again. Finally she let me go, with the weight of the world off my shoulders.

For a number of days though, I held my breath every time our phone rang but as far as I know Annie O'Neil never did call my Mother. The lesson was well learned and kept me on the straight and narrow, well, for least a year or so. Then, that Little Devil once again whispered from my shoulder showering me with temptation! I had told Norman about being caught at O'Neil's and we decided it happened because the Store was too small! So after discussing it at length, we came up with a plan. It was at the University Plaza where we began a shoplifting spree that seemed to run quite well at least for a few days.

At first, we had stolen a number of items such as Candy Bars from the Drug Store which had been stashed in a cache we made in the woods behind the Plaza. Aikenhead's Hardware Store was next on the list and I recall removing a Dinky Toy from its box and putting it in my pants pocket. I don't recall what Norman took but we actually had made it out of the store when disaster struck! A hole in my pocket ripped open wider and this toy started to slide down my leg!! I struggled with awkward gestures to keep it from sliding out but we were right in front of the store window in full view!!

A Man from the Hardware Store was standing in there talking with someone and saw me through the front window. With the situation looking rather obvious, he bolted towards the door and we took off running now! Unfortunately, we didn't get very far and were quickly apprehended and marched back to the store by the scruff of our necks and taken to a back office. Soon, a Police Officer arrived and we were made to empty our pockets. Next came the question, had we stolen anything from any other store? We replied in unison, No from Norman and Yes from me and I spilled my guts about the hidden cache as well! The Officer escorted us back to the woods retrieving our stash.

Now passengers in the Police Cruiser, we were driven over to the Dundas Driving Park, where he pulled over and began the significant questioning. I can still hear him drone on with the questions. Who else was involved, nobody. "What is your alias?? What does that mean? Oh, Al I guess". On it went as He filled in a long legal size form. Then the agonizing short drive over to my house first where I knew that Mini King Kong was waiting as she had already been called. I figured "the Belt or Ironing Cord lashes" would follow but this time it was different!

She lit into me roaring it was the last straw this time!! Down the Hall she went grabbing 3 of those old-fashioned brown paper shopping bags with twine handles. Then up the stairs to my room with me following pleading for forgiveness! I watched transfixed as she emptied my Dresser Drawers one at a time stuffing my clothes and filling the bags until the Dresser was empty!

Now taking them downstairs, she picked up the phone and dialed the Police telling them I was ready to be picked up!! Just as Annie O'Neil had forewarned, I was told they'd be taking me away to Reform School!! She took a Kitchen Chair and made me sit at the front door with my clothes advising that you weren't allowed to take toys or anything else. As I sat there waiting, I imagined all kinds of horrors I would soon encounter.

She made me sit there a long time noting that the Police must be busy! Later on she came with another chair and sat down beside me and said she might reconsider if I could promise to be very good in the future! Of course at that point I would have taken 50 lashes!! After considering it for a few minutes she called the Police back advising them she had changed her mind.

Now I know obviously she hadn't called the Police but this young boy certainly bought it, lock, stock and barrel! I also think in retrospect that Norman and I probably blamed each other for instigating this mini-crime spree as for the umpteenth time we were not allowed to play with each other. So we didn't at least while our Parents were paying attention to our whereabouts and of course we still were in School together!

Luckily for us as well in retrospect, we never heard again from the Police, as obviously no charges from the stores were made! A number of years later then a young man, I dropped into O'Neil's advising Annie who I was and thanked her for her long-ago lesson and kindness. She remembered and was happy that I had eventually grown up to be responsible. I wonder how many other "bad" kids might have received that lecture! As Kids, we only knew Annie for her store, Candy and Comic Books.

As noted in Dundas History though, she was much more than a shopkeeper. She was an astute Business Woman, Town Councilor and a Pillar of the community who has and will continue to be long remembered.

Chapter Twenty-One

Working Boys

There comes a time in a young Boy's Life where the gap between your allowance and your spending requirements becomes so large that you have to find other ways to support your income. While my friends and I briefly dabbled in snow shoveling, it wasn't required every week so we had to come up with other ideas. I remember reading about Cowboys who back in the day, "hired on for $30 a month and found". The pay of course, included a bed in a Bunk House, meals and the occasional "found" like an unbranded Steer you could sell to the Rancher.

To us, "found" was a slightly different description and one of the earliest ventures I recall was "finding" grapes. We didn't have to go to Vineland either as there were two small vineyards we discovered in Dundas. One was at the top of the Hill above the Golf Course just past what is known as the entrance to the Grand Vista Subdivision. For us it was a dangerous venture as the owner was known to be vigilant over his crop.

The first time I heard the shotgun blast, it scared the bejesus out of me! I think I could have set an Olympic Record running out of there. Later I learned that some kids had actually been shot with rock salt! We weren't exactly sure what rock salt was but had heard it was painful but you couldn't get killed!! How comforting! We still snuck back there a few times though a frantically quick Harvest in the darkness failed to yield much.

Later on we found another crop just up the hill from the Parkside High School and not patrolled with a shotgun or even monitored! Very nice plump Green Grapes and we took our share of the harvest in pillowcases. Later, I was complicit in the disappearance of a number of one-quart wooden baskets from our house much to my

Mother's dismay as they went missing. Filling them and Loading them in a wagon, we young entrepreneurs went merrily along our way, knocking on doors a number of blocks away from our neighborhood selling this high-quality fruit at great prices to grateful Customers! The Sales pitch of course was that our Father having an overabundance of grapes, had sent us out to sell them. That worked well and I while I imagine some heads shaking here, we only did it a few times, honest! Just like snow though, it didn't last.

Next came the paper route, the Hamilton Spectator's which I picked up from Jaggards Store and later on Park Street near Sydenham. 68 of them, down Park Street, up the York Road to the Cemetery Gates then down East Street into the survey of Concord and Cameron Streets.

Jaggard's News Agency circa 1930

Photo Val Harvey Patterson

6 Days a week and on Saturdays, huge and heavy! When it came to Veteran Newspaper Boys, Willie Aitkens was a Dundas Legend and had a heavy-duty bicycle with a custom-like basket I always envied. He trundled around Dundas for years delivering his papers.

I can still see him pedaling away in his black white topped running shoes and Glasses wearing a plaid shirt, tails flapping away. It was quite sad when he mysteriously passed away years later in the Dundas Quarry.

Photo Val Harvey Patterson

As I recall, I had to pay the Newspaper about 18-20 dollars a week and the profit margin wasn't high. This was compounded occasionally when trying to collect folk's subscription payments. As a Carrier, you had to pay the Newspaper the full amount regardless of what you had collected and my Mother had to occasionally subsidize that cost. For some customers you'd have to go back several times to find them home to collect. As well, I had a few "Shade Peekers" where you would knock on the Door and see a window shade raise slightly but no one would answer and it took a number of weeks to finally get paid. I'd retaliate by not dropping a good Saturday Paper but all that got me was a complaint and an order to deliver one back toot sweet! The Cream of the Crop Routes were those with Apartment Buildings like near University Plaza where you could drop a lot of papers with little effort. I wasn't so lucky but I did have a smaller building at 89 York Road which I appreciated. Christmas was good though when many folks showed their appreciation for your reliability.

Before the University Plaza location, the Dundas Bowling Alleys were on Foundry Street just down from our original house, back of the Post Office and the other down at the foot of the 102 Hwy (Cootes Drive). It would later become the Rose and Thistle. I don't think I was ever in the one on Foundry Street, though I do remember that an Architectural Firm bought the building years later and received an award for how they utilized the original "Bowling Lanes" to create the floors for their offices.

I did though get a job, setting up Pins at the lanes down at the end of the 102 Hwy. I struggle now to remember its name but perhaps it was Sam's. Anyway, I can still see the Manager or Owner; I remember we called him Big John and I picture him with his large black framed glasses. I set the bowling pins for 5-pin games and once shown what to do, it was ridiculously easy. They'd roll the balls, knock down the pins and you'd gather them up from a trough at the end of the lane. Then stepping down on a metal plate which popped up spikes you would drop a pin on each spike to steady and put them in the perfect alignment. Then, taking your foot off the peddle, the spikes would drop and you would climb back up on a raised bench and wait for them to be knocked over again.

Easy right? Little did I know of the hazards of the occupation. I remember the first night it happened when one of my Veteran Co-workers suddenly had this urge to go pee so I took over his lane. Now relaxing there like a sitting Duck there was this deafening crash as a ball flew down the lane at a hurricane-like speed and launched the pins!!. One hit me mid-section knocking the wind out of me while another just missed my head. There was this Giant of a Man hurling these bowling balls down the lane. My Co-Workers were in hysterics!! My life was threatened for a crummy 15 cents a game!!! Time for other endeavors.

My next pursued occupation was Golf Caddying. My Brother Billy was an 'A" Caddy at the Dundas Golf and Country Club. I wasn't good enough for there so I plied my trade at the Beverly Golf Club up in Flamboro with some friends and we used to hitchhike up there just off Christie's Corners on Hwy 8. If you've ever seen the film, "The Caddy" with Jerry Lewis, that was me! Check out the YouTube Link for it. I didn't get to Caddy for Dean Martin either it was usually Fat Old Ladies who knocked the ball about 20 feet with each swing.

There were very few carts then too and sometimes I had to struggle with a Golf Bag larger than me. Given those Golfer's distance limitations, you'd be out there in the blazing Sun for hours. The Beverly Golf Club was beautiful but it was at the end of the day, in the middle of the Beverly Swamp!! Home to a number of slimy and scary things like snakes.

Now these Golfers had some other challenges too like hitting the ball straight down the fairway and often when they did it wasn't much past 50 feet or so. When it went into the swamp you were expected to go in there and retrieve it. "Caddy, would you please try to find my ball in there?" Right!! I used to carry a couple of balls in my pocket, one white and one pink which was the colour of choice for ladies. This allowed me to find balls fast without an Everglades-like journey.

"Here it is, got it" as I drew it from my pocket! Occasionally they'd check the ball announcing it wasn't their's and my jungle expedition would resume. All of this adventure at 75 cents for 9 holes or around 2 bucks for 18. I started to have fond memories of the Bowling Alley at least it was comfortable and with no snakes!

Dave Hood my almost Step Father had won the "500 Dollar Draw" at the Legion and bought a small Bunkie like Cottage at Featherstone Point on Lake Erie. Close by was the small Town of Fisherville where I acquired new Friends during the summers. It was close by there where I got a Farm Job one year. In the fall collecting Hay Bales. My first lesson was never to wear a short sleeve shirt doing that job. My forearms looked like I tried to separate 4 Cats in a fight, scratched all to hell.

It was an interesting job for a novice Farm Boy, we'd drive a Tractor thru the field pulling a trailer and loading it with Hay Bales. Now, back at the Barn we would put the bales on a Hay Escalator to someone up in the loft of the Barn to stack them. A Hay Escalator basically works the same way as the one at the Mall. It was however extremely old and kept slipping out of gear. I would have to jump down off the wagon and push the vertical lever back in to start it moving again. After having to do this several times, I got frustrated and jumping down, kicked the handle which resulted in a pile of gears bouncing across the ground causing the operation of the equipment to abruptly stop. My Boss the Owner of the Farm was not impressed though after some tinkering managed to get it going again.

Though I managed to survive this indiscretion, another issue occurred shortly thereafter. When throwing Hay Bales about, a necessary tool is the Bale Hook, a large Captain Hook like tool which allowed you to firmly grasp a hay bale to throw it. While that tool worked well I tossed it away at some point to the ground. Shortly thereafter we drove over it puncturing the large rear tire.

That ended my Farm Boy career and my earnings after the Escalator repair and Tractor Tire Plug were not considerably sufficient to compensate for my suffering!

Chapter Twenty-Two

Dog Days of Summer

The Dog Days of Summer is a phrase from Astronomy, which relates to the Canis Major (Greater Dog) Constellation, near Sirius, the Brightest Star which rises at the start of the Hot Sultry days of summer. As I am certainly not a Weather or Meteorology Geek, you can look up the rest on your own but the Dog Days of Summer are from July 3rd thru August 11th. For our reference here, it was the days in Dundas back in the day when it was damn hot!

That being said, it's not like it isn't hot now by any means, in fact it is, as we all know with Global Warming, significantly hotter for sure. Back then though as kids we all managed to survive, without Air Conditioning! As a kid from my recollection, the only place I remember in Dundas having Air Conditioning was the Deluxe Restaurant and I wasn't supposed to go there at least while anyone was looking. I think it also may have been Air Conditioned in the Roxy Movie Theatre as well.

The two places where I suffered the most were our Family Home and St. Augustine's School. Our former House on Melville Street in the Heritage District was well over 100 years old and the upstairs bedrooms were constructed in the Dormer style which means slanted ceilings following the outline of the Roof. Though I am sure the lower level of the House accessed from Sydenham Street was likely cooler, our living area on Melville Street was like a sweatbox on those Hot Summer Days!

Upstairs, the Sun beat down on that roof all day until you could have baked a cake up there. Though I loved my Mother dearly, there were times when I ....well let's just say we had our differing opinions. Going to bed upstairs at night was like climbing into an Oven. I can still hear her, "If you just lay still, you will be much cooler"! Right, I am sure if you were drugged and tied down that night it might be possible, but I died from the heat over and over on too many sleepless nights to count.

Even the effects of a Cold Bath quickly dissipated as you climbed the stairs to Hell!! Our Windows featured those 6-inch high screens which I am sure only let the hotter outside air in! We didn't own a Fan though they only push the hot air around anyway!

One day Dave our Senior Boarder gained my rapt attention telling me about what his Family did back in his day to cool a room in a house. You remember Dave; he was the one that taught our Budgie, Toby to swear! As he was born in 1911, I doubt that they even had a fan! Taking note of his detailed instructions, I grabbed the largest Cast Iron Frying Pan from our Pantry and cleaned out all of the Ice Cubes from our small Fridge Freezer.

As my Mother was occupied elsewhere I managed to get the material upstairs without being noticed. I then placed as many ice cubes as possible in the pan and poured water over top of them. Carefully, I removed the screen from my bedroom window and wrenched the Window up to the highest level possible. The idea was to then place the frying pan in the middle of the window ledge. The theory was that should there be any breeze outside it would flow in over the ice water and be cool!

It has always struck me as amazing in my life how theory and reality can often be so incredibly different. As for this inventive endeavor, in mere minutes after shutting the light off things went downhill rapidly! Firstly there was no breeze outside at all. Then the mosquitoes came in through the unscreened window. After a few minutes, the Window came crashing down on the frying pan making a loud banging noise and some ice cubes with some water dropped and slid down to the linoleum-covered floor. Then came the familiar yell from downstairs, "What's' going on up there".

Now as I hurriedly tried to ditch the evidence, I lifted the window up and the frying pan slid off the ledge dropping 10-12 feet or so down the outside of the House!! After explaining why it wasn't my fault, I still got in big trouble though at least this time I had a partner in crime to share my Mother's wrath!

Back then, Swimming Pools were a luxury and there were a few private ones maintained by wealthy Residents in Dundas. For the general public however, there was only one outdoor pool operated by the Lions Club next to the Arena. I got to go there regularly until the day of the huge controversy! There was an article in the Dundas Star, circa early 60's about a Water Test that had been conducted there which resulted in the discovery that there was a very large percentage of urine in the water!! After my Mother read that, the Lions Pool was added to the banned locations list!

That resulted in many a visit to Dundas's well-known Swimming Hole in the Spencer Creek under the Hope Street Bridge. While I am sure some urine likely escaped one's shorts there too, at least the water was moving. As there was no Johnny on the spot then, you had to watch carefully where you walked too as most Kids found it too far to go home for the bathroom and such urges were addressed there. I also remember swinging off some vines from the Trees into the Creek off the 102 (Cootes Dr.) but the creek water there was murky with a mucky bottom. With all of the Snakes and Snapping Turtles down there, uptown Hope Street was my preference though it was often crowded.

At St. Augustine's School, back then it was a sweatbox on those hot fall days. During recess or lunch at least in my early days there, you weren't allowed to go back into the school for a drink for some reason. I ended up drinking water from the creek down Alma Street near the Park which resulted in a severe bout of Kidney Disease which I fortunately recovered from. A Diet of Dry Toast was prescribed for several weeks, with no butter or jam, yuck!

I wonder if kids today still experiment trying to fry an Egg on the Sidewalk. What I lacked in scientific knowledge was aided greatly by my imagination! I reasoned that if the egg didn't sizzle on one sidewalk slab, it might be on the next one! It was certainly something

I tried to do a number of times on boiling hot summer days. It never worked of course at least not for me with my limited patience and my Mother didn't appreciate an unplanned egg shortage or the mess on the Sidewalk in front of the House either!

Many years later, with my Mother now living alone in our Homestead, we'd go to visit regularly. When we'd go there in the hot summer weeks, just stepping inside the door was enough to ignite those memories of the evening heat misery of long ago. I decided to buy her a Window Air Conditioner which I installed in one of the front Living Room Windows. I turned it on and when we left an hour or so later it was getting really comfortable! The thing was though, every time we went back that summer, it was always turned off and there she would be in that Red Brick Sauna with a sweater on!

Looking back on it, I am sure many will remember their left-tanned forearms from it resting on the open Driver' window of the older Cars. As well as that wonderful wet back of your shirt stuck to your back from the simmering hot plastic upholstery of the Car Seat while sitting in rush hour traffic. How about dropping your swimming trunks over the aerial on the car which had them dry by the time you got home from the Lake? Though Air Conditioned Cars were rather expensive in the early years, once I bought one, I'd never have another without it.

Thinking about cars, here is a recollection that most folks will identify with, your first car! I will never forget mine, a faded Pukey lime green, 1959 Ford Fairlane. I bought it from a Man on the East Hamilton Mountain. One Hundred Dollars cash and no such thing as a safety certificate. I drove it away with the radio blasting in seventh heaven until I turned a corner and the radio fell out from under the Dashboard. I managed to wedge it back in.

Now to further personalize it, I added an 8 Ball to the end of the gear shift and a Chrome Footprint for the gas pedal. Next came tinted windows where I inhaled 3 cans of spray and stumbled around higher than a kite. That money would have been better spent buying tires with tread, they were so bald they looked like racing slicks.

Lastly was the Wolf Whistle that my Uncle gave me. It was a two-barrel whistle that was attached to the exhaust pipe with a wire to the Driver's seat. It was a relic from the Model T days. I would pull the wire closing it over the exhaust pipe making a shrill Calliope sound. It was quite the attention grabber. There weren't a lot of guys with a car then and it was a Chick Magnet and I was (so I thought) super cool. Cruising on a Friday Night, the popular locations were Harvey's Hamburgers on Main West just east of the University Plaza. It was take out only then and we sat on the hood of the car eating our burgers with Beach Boys and other songs of the day blasting out the car's open windows.

Alternatively, it was over to the A & W on Plains Road in Burlington. No speakers in those days, you had to turn on your headlights once ready to order. I also managed to acquire a number of those glass Root Beer Mugs. Later as I dated a few of those A&W Girls, I was shocked to learn that the cost of those missing mugs was deducted from their paychecks and I gave mine to one of those Girls to turn back in.

As you might imagine, access to a Car for an older Teenager launched a number of other exciting adventures. One night, I was parked in the Rock Chapel Lot above Dundas, um having a discussion of sorts with my Girl Friend of the time. Spying a Police Cruiser quietly pulling in the far entrance, I left in a hurry and halfway to Greensville was pulled over. The Officer asked me why I left and I said oh just going home. After having a look in my trunk, he let us go, fortunately I had no booze in the car.

One of my favorites related to my first car was the Drive-In Movie Theatre. There were 4 in this area in the 60's. The Clappison in the nearby Community of Waterdown and the Hamilton, Skyway and Starlite Drive-In's in Hamilton. Amazingly, many many years later, the Starlite Drive-In is still going strong on the East Hamilton Mountain. Most if not all were owned by the Dydzak Family. Drive-Ins of course were not known for featuring Academy Award Winning Films. They were however, less expensive outings that catered to young families who could bring their pajama-clad youngsters with their Teddy Bears and pillows and save Baby Sitter expenses. Though those Family outings were popular there occasionally would be an announcement overriding the film soundtrack which later in life, I once heard, "Would Mr. Duffin please come to the Snack Bar, your Son Bradley is waiting for you". That walk among all those Cars in the dark could be confusing.

Drive-Ins were also very popular with my generation and better known as the Passion Pit which um, well for me was more appropriate. Though the Clappison was slightly closer, my favorite was in Hamilton likely because it was the only Drive-In that also operated in the Winter providing you with an in-car heater as well as the speaker. More than occasionally, cars would drive away with the speaker still attached pulling the wires and disconnecting it from the post. These accidents though were cheerfully forgiven and you could turn the speaker back into the Snack Bar with no charge. Later on, speakers were discontinued in favor of a locally transmitted audio you could tune in on your car radio. Drive-Ins also featured a mechanically inclined staff member ready with Jumper Cables to assist those patrons whose batteries had run down during the evening. On Holiday Weekends Midnight Screenings were featured usually with Horror Films, usually 4 in a row.

I used to enjoy the intermission snack bar jingles and animation of Wieners jumping into Buns and the Grandmother ringing the bell reminding us there were only 3 minutes until showtime! You can still view these nostalgic features of long-ago theatres on line.

While Parents saved money on Baby Sitters, we had another innovative way ourselves of reducing costs. I certainly could not claim to be the initiator of the "Trunk In", though I will admit to practicing it occasionally. For us young guys to save money we would double date at the Drive-In and upon entry we'd all be in the car, though two of us would ride in the trunk. The Driver would pay the admission for him and his date, then drive to the back row and let the other couple out of the trunk. This was a popular practice though mine ended the time I was asked at the Ticket Booth to get out of the car and open my trunk! "Don and Linda now how'd you two get in there?" Right, well they still let us in after we paid the 4 admissions of course. Funny today in thinking about that, I couldn't do it now as I have acquired claustrophobic tendencies over the years.

As for that car, we parted company after a Telephone Pole got in my way beside Greensville's Tip Top Canners. My Face wasn't so pretty for 3 or 4 weeks and my Mother and Sister had to sit in the Court Room as the Judge christened me with a Drinking Under Age conviction. While I had missed out on the Ravine Bashes, the reward at least was comparable.

Chapter Twenty-Three

Suckers

Having lived away from Dundas for many years, it was interesting one day to read about the Dundas Sucker Festival created by Marty Zuliniak a number of years ago. I happened to discover an article about it in the Newspaper one day. It brought back memories of being down at the Spencer Creek with Marty and others back when we were kids; I remember a bunch of us netting suckers in the Creek during their spring spawn. I don't remember now who owned the net but what a number of us would do was to get into the creek.

Marty Zuliniak with Jack Johnston promoting the Sucker Derby

Photo courtesy of Zuliniak Family

I can see it in my mind now, the person holding the net would be downstream on the right-hand side and 2 or 3 of us would be up on the left waiting for a school of Suckers to appear. Once we saw it, wielding large tree saplings we would slap the water furiously driving the fish to the opposite side of the creek where the net awaited them not far downstream. Not all of them moved over though and it was the strangest feeling having them brush by your legs in large volumes. Then with a number of fish in the net, they would be dumped on the bank of the creek. I honestly cannot remember now what we did with them, but I didn't take any home.

My Brother had warned me that Mom wouldn't cook them as they are a bottom-feeding fish much like a Carp and also full of bones. Suckers are particularly tolerant to polluted water and with those well-designed lips they can literally vacuum the bottom of the creek and they will eat anything. All those lips needed were lipstick like those old Aunts we all had and cringed when you had to present yourself for the required sloppy smudge!! Anyway, my Mother had cautioned me that anyone who eats suckers gets to enjoy whatever they ate! Likely there is a good way to prepare and cook them but as a young Boy, I almost choked to death once on a fish bone.

Permanently wired from that experience, when I find myself in a situation of eating fish with bones, I chew it like an overzealous Cow until satisfied there are no bones present. By then of course it tastes like shredded cardboard and my appetite wanes significantly! I do enjoy eating Fish and Chips from the Shops dedicated to making it with no fear of bones. Our Family enjoyed our weekly order from the legendary Frosty's Fish and Chips a Dundas Landmark sadly no longer. So as Catholics of course our Family followed the rules for fish only on Fridays though occasionally I'd sneak over to the Deluxe for a Burger! Though the Catholic Church discontinued the Fish on Friday practice in the mid 80's, Fridays still remain the busiest day at all of the Fish and Chip Shops.

Chapter Twenty-Four

Rollers Skates and more Pranks

The Dundas Grightmire Arena was of course well known for Hockey and Skating but it was also a great Roller Skating Venue. I had forgotten about an abrupt end to a budding romance that happened there one evening. I was dating a young lady who was a Student Nurse at St. Joseph's School of Nursing in Hamilton. She was an avid Roller Skater and wanted to go skating one night at the Arena. I had never been on roller skates before but as I could skate on Ice, I presumed that it would be no different so we went over there and I rented my skates.

I remember I thought the atmosphere was cool with music and the throngs of people skating. While the skating motions are somewhat similar, I learned rather quickly that when it comes to stopping, there is a significant difference! I lost my balance, yanked her hand and she went flying. We left early after she ripped her slacks open at the knees, bruising and cutting them. Things kind of cooled off after this unfortunate incident but life went on and I guess that relationship simply wasn't meant to be. Funny though how holes in your jeans knees are quite fashionable today.

There are no doubt many Folks reading this who once played a neighborhood prank and some called it Nicky, Nicky, Nine Door where you would ring someone's doorbell then take off and watch from a distance as they answered the door, looking around. We had a bit of a different version where we would collect Dog Excrement in a small paper bag and put it on the doorstep lighting it on fire, then ring the doorbell and run! The Door would open and when seeing the fire on occasion someone would stamp their foot on it, making a mess. It was no fun if water was poured on it to put it out!! Other variations we sometimes employed were throwing a small water-filled balloon at someone as they opened the door or standing there and asking if

Mr. (dumb made-up name) was there. Of course given the strange name they never were and we likely would have ran away if someone ever said, yes, I'll go get him! Once they closed the door we would be in hysterics and run away.

I remember one night we were at the famous Walnut Cottage on Victoria Street. Norman was supposed to ask, "Is Mr. Walnut there?" I remember a Man with large framed glasses answered the door, but instead of asking for Mr. Walnut, Norman says "Is Mr. Grunt there?" at which we both cracked up laughing and running away with him yelling "I am calling the Police"! He did too and I came very close to getting caught having to lie under a Car in a Driveway off Cross Street looking at a Police Officer's Boots while trying not to breathe or make a sound!!

We often played on the Train Tracks up on the side of the Escarpment. We had heard how you could put your Ear to the Rail and if a Train was coming there would be a clicking sound. I remember us up there trying that one day. I heard absolutely nothing but I did look up to see a Train rapidly approaching which scared me good as we quickly scampered off the tracks.

Up where the Dundas Train Station used to be above District High School, there was also a nearby Supply Shed. One night we got in there and collected a number of track signals. They were a small paper-like square with a wire clip that allowed you to attach it to the Railway Track. It contained a small explosive charge and when the Train passed over it, it would make a loud bang like a gunshot. Presumably a number of them at a certain distance from the Train would alert the Engineer of a danger or an unscheduled stop.

While our supply lasted, we put a number of them on the track to hear the machine gun-like bangs for fun though the Trains never slowed down or stopped. One night behind the Arena, I remember a number of us trying to set one off with a Trailer Hitch when the Police arrived. Fortunately we all got away after being chased into the Spencer Creek by a Cop and climbing up the Hogs Back Hill!!

Coming home soaked later I can't recall now what story I told but as usual my Mother was not impressed.

Chapter Twenty-Five

Childhood Adventures

Though I am not aware of how popular chestnuts might be today, back in the 50's and 60's collecting them was a popular pastime. In Dundas there were numerous Chestnut Trees. Not to be confused with water chestnuts the culinary treat, these were horse chestnuts. Taking an old shoelace, the larger ones were drilled and you threaded the lace down thru it tying a knot to hold it in place. We called these conkers or kingers. The objective was to swing it hard against someone else's trying to smash it to pieces. You kept track of how many you destroyed if you had a hard nut. Large ones tended to last longer but were hard to find and those that fell from the tree on their own were usually too ripe to last long. Also some Kids soaked them too to add to their hardness.

So you threw balls or sticks up into the Tree to try to knock them down. I had the perfect stick for these, part of a thick tree branch that was hard and about a foot long. Checking out the trees you would look for large clumps of chestnuts. I am not sure if it's still there today but on the west side of Sydenham Road, just a few feet down from Melville Street there was a good Chestnut Tree, kind of behind the House on the northwest corner. Our House was the second one east of Sydenham on the right on Melville Street.

One day spying a good-sized clump, I let my stick fly with a perfect aim and got a great hit sending nuts flying. The problem was the stick kept flying thru the tree branches into one of the windows on the House with a loud crash. The mistake I made was running up to Melville and heading east to my house. This allowed the Man running from the house in question to catch me about 20 feet from my front door. My Mother responded to the pounding at the front door quite deafening to me.

There I dangled held by the scruff of the neck by an irate gentleman. She gladly paid for the window replacement which I unhappily financed from several allowances and of course a significant grounding.

Dundas back in the day was a smaller community than what exists today though not as small as you might think. From my recollection as a young boy I remember it being 12,000 then 14,000 for a number of years which were on population signs on the 102 (Cootes Drive). When our Town was finally amalgamated with the City of Hamilton I think it had grown to over 20,000. Given Dundas is partially surrounded by protected Green Spaces including the Dundas Valley Conservation Area, any further growth of the community will be hopefully limited and it will be able to maintain its small-town charm and feeling.

Frankly as in any Small Town where Kids are present, there will always be ample opportunity for public mischief. As many will recall, during the long-ago summer months, in most Households, Roll Call commenced once the Street Lights came on. Often, Search Parties comprised of older siblings were sent out to the usual known locations to track down the missing. I know for me on many a day, I was subsequently marched back to the House by my older Brother Billy who very much enjoyed providing the details of my capture to my Mother! One day he even ratted me out for smoking!

Of course his memory of such detail today regarding me is completely vague and he denies much of what I clearly remember in particular that I learned from him, like those Milk Bottle withdrawals. I'll also bet he has forgotten the Streetlight that was a mere 20 feet down Melville Street from the House. It was a single bulb style covered by a flat circular metal disk-like fixture. He showed me how to take a large rubber band and a Bobby Pin and after a few attempts, a direct hit on the Bulb would take it out with a flash and shower of sparks. I'd conduct that challenge a couple of times per year for a few years and I wonder what the Hydro Guys thought finding it shattered each time an inspection took place.

One Fall Night my friend Norman and I had gone into St. Augustine's Church after dinner and no one was there so we were looking around when we suddenly heard the Front Door open so we hid in a washroom near the front door. It must have been one of the Priests and we heard his footsteps while he walked about sliding bolts and pulling chains on the massive doors to lock them for the night. Here we were, now locked in the Church and though we tried we couldn't get any of the large front Doors open!!

So, taking the next logical step as curious teenagers now having the run of the place, we decided to go up in the balcony. Our first thought was to ring the large bell but we didn't know how to do that so we went over to the Organ! We turned it on and pressed some keys down and a scary like wail thundered throughout the Church and we took off downstairs and found a door out behind the front Altar. We held our breath for a few days but never heard anything about it but then again we never damaged anything.

The Alleyway behind the Deluxe Restaurant was another area we'd hang out in after dark and behind the Restaurant was a circular stone walled garden. One night we armed ourselves with some overripe tomatoes and oranges from the garbage there. We banged on the back door of the Restaurant, Du Wong stepped out in his white Chef's attire and we let fruit fly at him yelling what would be now considered politically incorrect insults at him!! Yelling blue murder at us he'd chase us down the alley Meat Clever in hand.

One night as I was making a quick getaway thru a back fence of a Park Street House, my shoe got caught in a hole in the fence!! Terrified, I yanked and yanked my leg until it came free but my shoe came off but I ran anyway. Now of course as my luck would have it, my Mother happened to meet me at the front door and of course immediately noticed my shoe was missing. I made up a story about minding my own business when Mr. Wong came out and chased us. I refused to go back and finally my Mother sent my Brother to retrieve it after I described where it was. I had also torn my pant leg and gouged my leg well on the broken fence wood which wasn't appreciated by her either!

One year, perhaps inspired by Robin Hood on T.V., a bunch of us got fiberglass Bows and a bunch of those dull-tipped arrows. I remember we tried to hunt squirrels with them though even if you got a direct hit they never penetrated anyway. We used to spend a lot of time in what we called the Cross Street Woods behind the Houses a block or so down from the Driving Park. One time having lost 3 arrows up in one tree there we decided to cut it down to retrieve the arrows.

It wasn't a large tree, perhaps 10-12 feet or so high and the trunk was only 6-7 inches thick. Working with an Axe and Saw we toiled away and it was close to an hour before it finally fell with a crash. An angry man stormed out of the back of the nearby House and quickly retrieving our arrows we took off with him in a hot pursuit but at a distance far enough for us to escape.

Another time, we discovered a Bull Dozer up on Helen Street off the Dundas Driving Park. It had been clearing the land for what would later become an Apartment Building. We had been playing on it pulling and twisting it's levers and gears when I noticed a button and pushed it! It roared to life scaring us good and it slowly began to move and we jumped off quickly running down the hill into the Park. I think it ended up stopping against a foundation or something and fortunately no damage was done.

Chapter Twenty-Six

Under Cover in the Dark

So on the north section of Elgin Street behind St. Augustine's Church, there is a House that back in the day at least, had a Swimming Pool in the backyard. On Summer Nights especially on Fridays and Saturdays we were given a little more leash-free time to be out after dark. I remember a few Pool Parties being thrown at that House and probably being attracted by the noise, two adventurous Boys snuck up to the back fence one night to have a look. Quickly over the fence and behind a cabana-like tent. My Friend being curious lifted a back flap on slightly to see what was inside and he sure spent a long time looking. Finally I pulled him back so I too could have a look.

Wow, it was a Change Tent and um, well you likely have grasped by now what we were looking at!! It truly was an anatomical education of sorts for us. Anyway, we went back to my Friends place where we had a tub where we had stashed some Suckers earlier in the day caught in the Spencer Creek. They were dead but still reasonably fresh so we took a few of them and snuck back behind the backyard fence. On the count of 3 we flung them high up over the fence and heard them splash in the pool and the screams that followed and boy did we take off running!!! I apologize now to anyone reading this if you were there but at least we did liven up the party!!

The following is a recollection of an event that occurred over 55 years ago in the absence of any motion detectors or related alarm systems and is definitely not recommended today. As many of you will remember, at Elementary Schools often Balls would leave the playground and end up on the School Roof, never to be seen again! I had often given this some thought in that there must be some way to get up there and get them.

There was an alleyway that ran from Alma Street across from St. Augustine's down to Victoria Street which many of us cut through on the way home. It was a well-travelled shortcut and also a staging ground for many a schoolyard like fight as well on occasion. Today of course it is no longer a thoroughfare having been closed off in recent years. One day walking down the lane on our way home from School, Norman and I noticed a Garage with its door open and saw a ladder hanging in there. Well of course, we took note of this and the following Saturday we sauntered over there in the dark and as luck would have it, the Garage Door was open! As the Coast was clear, we borrowed that Ladder which was a wooden 8-footer with an extension and we quickly lugged it across the playground and around the back of the school!

Up we went onto the East side of the School Roof at the back pulling the ladder up there with us. There had to be over 20 Balls of varying descriptions up there! We gathered up the good ones and tossed them down into the wooded area behind the School to be retrieved at a later time. So as we were already up there we decided to do some exploring and using the ladder again we went up to one level higher and walked along.

The original Front of St. Augustine's School had kind of reminded me of the Alamo, so I wanted to go over there to have a look around. Suddenly we came upon a square black cap of sorts that had to be investigated. We lifted it off and a few feet below there was another large square-like entrance lid. It easily lifted up and there was a dark hole and you could hear the heating system running below, a way into the School! Quickly back we went and pulled the ladder up again to bring it over. Now we carefully lowered the ladder into this black void until it stopped against a solid surface.

Norman went down first and as he disappeared into the blackness, the ladder suddenly dropped away from my hands. There was a crash followed by dead silence!! "Norman, Norman" I whispered then louder and a groan from down there followed. Then a light came on and I saw what had happened. There was a Card Table set up that the ladder had rested on and as he went down, one of the legs gave out, collapsing the table and dropping the ladder with it. He set up the table again and once again with the ladder now secured down I went and we quickly shut off the light. For any St. Augustine Alumni, the room we were in must have been the original School Office upstairs in the old section.

We went exploring down the dim hallway and worked our way around to the newer section. We stepped into one of the playground-facing classrooms and he told me how you can quickly flick a fluorescent light switch off and on so fast that the lights wouldn't come on. I say okay do it and he flicks the switch and of course, the lights come on with daylight like brilliance which he quickly shuts off but for anyone looking towards the school it would have shown like a beacon!! We go roaring down the hallway back to the ladder, up and out of there taking the ladder with us, which we still needed to get back to the ground again.

So we lay down peering over the edge and wait holding our breath to see if we have been discovered. The stillness of the night continued so we worked our way back across the sections of the roof and climbed down at the back again. I was so disappointed; I had planned to print some large insults about a few Teachers on some Blackboards with Chalk! It would have been so much fun when the questions started on the following Monday. We decided to return the ladder back to the Garage where we had borrowed it from for a reason I no longer remember now. A few days later my Mother did have some questions on where a few Balls came from and I explained how workers fixing the roof of the School had tossed them down to us! We kept those we wanted and gave the rest away to some friends though not telling anyone where we found them.

Chapter Twenty-Seven

Gunpowder and Cannons

My Friend's Father worked in the lab at the Steel Company. In one corner of the basement in their house was a bit of a lab and workshop of sorts. A few books as well sat on a counter and in one we discovered the ingredients that were mixed to create gunpowder and not as intricate as you might imagine.

As I am not allowed to tell Grandchildren many of these tales for obvious reasons I won't repeat that recipe here either but to say that the two major ingredients can be found in your local drug store. The Druggist at Ralph's Drug Store squinting over his bifocals at us asks, "What do you want this for"? When in doubt you could usually pass with "We are doing a school project". This time however he wasn't buying it though we did manage to leave with one of the ingredients we sought. Fortunately, Dundas then had two Drug Stores, Ralphs across from the Post Office and the IDA farther downtown on King St.

We obtained our second required ingredient with no questions asked there. Now allowances then didn't go far but we did manage to buy a bag of charcoal pieces. This is important and after pounding that bag numerous times with a baseball bat you get that nice charcoal powder to mix stuff with. Next with Sweet Heart Straws stolen from the Deluxe Restaurant we made wicks.

Around our house we had a number of old tins, the cardboard kind with metal tops and bottoms perhaps originally filled with Epsom salts or something like that. If you push down on the lid of those cans, it snaps closed tightly. So we took our newly manufactured gunpowder and one of those tins with a hole poked in the middle of the lid down to our favorite Alleyway behind the Deluxe Restaurant. Now inserting the wick into the can which we had placed on the ground we lit it with a match and ran like hell anticipating a loud explosion. What happened though was that the force blew the lid off and it showered up briefly like a firework and though flashy it had no appreciative sound at all. We were to say the least really disappointed.

A few months later in the fall I happened to come across an article in an encyclopedia about old cannons. The principle is pretty basic with barrels of varying lengths and a wick hole at the back end. You place the wick in down the hole. Then push in what is called a charge followed by a projectile. Today when you see these old cannons it appears most if not all have had their barrels capped rendering them un-fireable for obvious reasons. However back in the day, not all of them were plugged.

In the minds of many folk's living in this area, the word Cannon associated with Dundas would likely generate memories of perhaps two locations. Perhaps by the Legion but likely that behemoth resting off the front of our old Town Hall. I did have a connection to that piece now buried within our family's photo vault someplace as a toddler straddling the barrel. The thought of trying to fire it though being so large and near the doorstep of the Police Station was strictly out of the question.

There was however another location literally across the street. On the southeast corner of Main and Dundas Streets today stands the Centurion Apartment Building. Back in the day though a large House (Stone Wall House) sat on a hill there supported by a stone retainer wall, I am sure a number of folks reading this will recall that. In remembering that House, I honestly cannot recall if we knew anyone who lived there or how we knew or discovered a small cannon perhaps 3 feet long sitting on its front lawn, but there it was resting upon a concrete mount. So we set about our plan with great zeal that would have been a highly regarded school project, well maybe.

You can imagine if we'd knocked on the door and asked if they would mind us firing their cannon so that was not an option. We did spend though a long time wiggling a metal coat hanger which we had pulled apart and straightened down the wick hole and bending it into the barrel in the dark of course the first night. While my Mother wondered what had happened to my ugliest pair of socks, we did fill one with our magic powder.

As noted after clearing the wick hole, we slid the Sweet Heart Straw down it. Using a plastic Lido Baseball Bat handle we shoved the ugly sock full of our homemade gunpowder down the barrel as tight as possible. Now what to use as the projectile? Being fall we rammed a pile of chestnuts in the barrel with the bat handle.

Demonstrating our brilliance or lack thereof, we lit the fuse, standing there a few feet away. The funny thing was for a few moments, nothing happened. Then suddenly with a bang, the chestnuts and owner of the House came roaring out. The explosion lifted the Cannon Barrel up out of the concrete base. That Man must have been an athlete. No one had ever chased us as many blocks as he did. Fortunately we escaped. Today I understand that cannon is sitting on a Front Lawn a mile or so away and is plugged.

Chapter Twenty-Eight

Soldiers

The 8th Field Regiment, 102nd Battery (Wentworth) was created from the Hamilton 11th Battery which was mobilized for WW11 in 1940. On D-Day, June 6th, 1944 The 11th Battery was the only Hamilton Unit to play a role in the landing of the Allied Forces in Normandy. It fired it's Guns in support of the Royal Winnipeg Rifles engaging German Defensive positions at point blank range and saw significant action supporting many other Divisions fighting their way through Normandy to the Rhine River. It was also the first Canadian Artillery Unit to actually cross the Rhine River into Germany.

It continued its war time activity under the Motto of the Royal Canadian Artillery, **Everywhere, whither right and glory lead**. At the conclusion of WW11 it returned to Hamilton to become part of the 8th Field Regiment Militia as the 40th Battery. It was split into two with the creation of the 102nd Wentworth Battery in Dundas. This Unit operating out of the Dundas Armories where it remained until relocated to Guelph in 1970. Continuing to seek adventure, I joined the 102 Battery Militia with a number of other Dundas Boys in the mid 60's.

Now this would be something we thought close to being a real Soldier with Rifles and real Cannons. In the Army Infantry, an ordinary Soldier has the rank of Private. In the Artillery Battery, you are a "Gunner". Little did we know though of the discipline and responsibilities soon to be instilled in us. Though Webster's Dictionary describes a Howitzer as a medium sized cannon that fired a projectile, we learned very quickly that the term cannon at least in the Canadian Army went out with the 19th century.

Gunner Duffin

In the 102nd Battery, we did indeed have Howitzers and they fired but it wasn't by lighting fuses as I had once experienced in the long ago prank. When we joined up initially, we were not allowed near them and it was a boot camp like atmosphere. Severe Discipline was thrust upon us unruly teenagers and we were marched endlessly around the Dundas Armories, now the Lion's Club Hall. Someone reading this might remember our beloved Drill Sergeant or Corporal and they could order you to do just about anything. That was bad enough but he was a short little bespectacled dude with his nose 1 inch from your chin and loudly yelling at you!! I can still hear him roaring "Gunner Duffin are you showing anger?" NO Sergeant!!! I bellowed back while I fantasized about decapitating him.

We also were outfitted with rifles too, FNC1's which were originally made in Belgium and gas-operated. It had a magazine which normally was loaded with blanks but there also were some live round shells for controlled firing at targets. Blank Shells have no lead and the ends of the shell casing are pinched together. Some Guys would take a nail to pry it slightly open and put a small stone fragment in there and pinch it closed to give whoever they pointed the rifle at a good sting if hit!! While we couldn't wait to fire them with the real shells, when we did get the chance our once rosy cheek began to look like a slab of beefsteak from its recoil.

To us former imaginary soldiers it was a gun but as any of your former Gunners out there, will remember, if you called it that you'd get in trouble!! Then you would be standing out on the Parade Square thrusting the RIFLE outward and chanting, "This is my Rifle" and pointing it at the Howitzer "That is my gun". Here I was, "Jerry Lewis" like again managing to get in trouble constantly but I certainly wasn't the only one.

Another infraction punishment the Drill Sergeant enjoyed was making you run around the Parade Square carrying your Rifle in front or over your head. It quickly became heavy and you had to keep running until you were ready to drop. So I ran, fantasizing this time of simply shooting him!! A less demanding though degrading task was cleaning urinals and/or the Armory Floor with a toothbrush which we were also rewarded with on occasion.

Our uniforms were the standard lime colour and itchy as hell but I guess they designed to keep you warm and less noticeable. Picture 2 Gunners in front of me trying to tie my uniform tie too which I always had difficulty with. So you suited up and finished it off with a Forge Cap (see photo). The Boots!! Well how could I forget them? I mean we had to polish them in Sea Cadets but in the Army it was borderline fanatical how they were expected to shine like a mirror. On issue they were this dull finished black leather with millions of tiny bubble-like indentations. Today they heat spoons to do drugs but back then we'd heat a spoon to press down and flatten those indentations on the boot. Eventually with significant effort you could shine them up well, just in time too to slog thru the mud on maneuvers.

In order to effectively fire one of those Howitzers, it required a 7-man crew. Positions 4, 5, 6, and 7 swung the Gun around in a direction as ordered by the Number 1. Members 2 and 3 sighted the aim so to speak, raising or lowering the barrel as directed and also loading the charge and shell.

After being aimed and loaded, a cord was yanked which caused the gun to fire! When it did it, the Howitzer jumped with its wheels rising off the ground. A burning hot shell casing was ejected then requiring a reload etc. A number of us novices suffered from burned hands touching these shell casings. Now reasonably trained we were considered ready for the upcoming War Games to be staged. It was on a weekend against Hamilton's Argyle and Sutherland Unit at Canadian Forces Base, Meaford or Borden. Some trips were also made by Air to Shiloh, north of Winnipeg on occasion.

The Quarter Master's store is the Military Supply Depot and we were sent there to be outfitted for these field maneuvers, a large Duffel bag filled with all the goodies including a field mess (metal eating containers) kit etc. In the Army you only go by the nickname bestowed upon you by your squad members. "Muffin Duffin" as Marty Zuliniak had christened me with a Bruce Ralston chorus, "Have you seen the Muffin Man?"

But what you do learn very quickly is the serial number assigned to you which is just as important or perhaps more so than your name and is recorded for every item provided to you. So here we are in a line to be issued our gear. Chuck Taylor is in front of me and is suddenly thrown out and whispers to me, "I forgot my serial number". Oh oh, I didn't remember mine either and I had to think fast!! So I walk in at my turn and the number is demanded and I say "Serial Number, oh I haven't been issued one yet", right!! I too am literally thrown out of there quickly!! By the way, that number, B-823796 I have always remembered since.

Though they did eventually issue our gear after a severe tongue-lashing (all Sergeants loved screaming at you) we did of course get punished again. I recall we were posted to guard our vehicles while everyone else ate Dinner. That didn't go well either as someone from the enemy in a similar uniform and with Fake Orders shown to us, stole a Truck. Those Trucks were affectionately known as Duce and halves given their 2.5 ton weight and with the Military's seating capacity of **"always one more** "they crammed us in there, but it beat walking. At Meaford once, a Tank near us fired and I swear that heavy truck left the ground from the concussion and you could literally feel the "Thump" in your chest as our butts left the bench seats!

As for allowing a Truck to be stolen, no one had cautioned us that this might happen and the 102nd lost some score from the maneuver over it. Chuck and I of course continued in the Dog House for the rest of the weekend. It was winter and freezing cold outside and one of the boys had also supplied a number of us with a number of bottles of homemade wine drained from their Father's Barrel! Donny Kolenski maybe, I can't remember but there was ample room to stash these old liquor bottles full of it in those duffel bags. Yes Sir, and also ample fortification for that cold weather. I can still see my Friend Bruce hurling a projectile-like stream, filling his boots with it from the top bunk!

Guard Duty was also a requirement during the night to keep an eye out for possible enemy attacks. A schedule was laid out for a number of Gunners, maybe an hour or so each and included me of course. When it was my turn, I remember going out for about 10 minutes. The hell with that, it was freezing so I snuck back in and woke up some other unsuspecting Gunner, telling him it was his turn then jumped back in bed.

Now just imagine a 6 a.m. roll call with a number of young Soldiers suffering horrible hangovers from guzzling that Homemade Vino the night before. You came very quickly after being ordered up and out of the barracks into an unheated Shower Hut with only ice-cold water. A 2-minute time slot was allowed for each shower each to scrub your frozen naked body with a communal plain bar of soap and a quick rinse. If you went over that time allotted, they yanked you out of the shower!

Now we filled ourselves with nice warm breakfast chow followed by more parading around during the day but with darkness approaching the battle time would be soon. The information was all provided to our 102nd battery and the Argyll's (the enemy) as they were called through map grid references. Though we considered Kilt wearing Bagpipers by us, we soon learned that the Argylls were a formidable force!!

So with 2 or 3 Howitzers we established a gun position on a small bluff. A small skirmish squad including me was sent out on a patrol, a cross between Hogan's Heroes and F Troop, they heard us laughing and arguing long before walking into a perfectly staged ambush! A bright flare or two sufficiently illuminated us and we experienced a heavy-fire assault that had it been real would have easily killed us all.

The following year, I had signed up for another 6-week maneuver somewhere and a few days before suffered a bout of mumps. Dr. Gow, my Family Doctor on Sydenham Street was an old Army Doctor too and managed to get me released from the commitment but fully paid at around 250.00 which was like winning the lottery then!

The Dundas Armory was constructed in 1874. Recently I discovered my Grand Father's enlistment document shown here and I had no idea he signed up at Dundas.

It was 1915 in a recruitment drive for the Great Canadian Expeditionary Force, our then fledgling Canadian Armed Forces.

He was unemployed at the time and it was the pay that originally had drawn him there to sign up. It was the day after my Mother's 3rd Birthday and the pay started immediately.

Library and Archives Canada

He went on to fight at Vimy Ridge. The 86th Machine Gunners Battalion became a reinforcement group dispersing soldiers to other units on the Front Lines as required. As a small boy I recall him showing me his honeycomb-like burn scars on his forearms from the Mustard Gas the German's had launched at them in canisters as they fought their way up and over Vimy Ridge where the French and British Forces had previously failed to advance.

Canadian Soldiers March to Vimy Ridge
Library and Archives Canada

As for those Kilts and Bag Pipes, those Pipers led the assault with no weapons and played on to inspire our advancing troops! From my Grandfather's description of it, the German Soldiers were amazed and terrified at this spectacle. They called them **"The Ladies from Hell"** as they led the troops marching in their kilts and playing this strange music! Looking at this document and remembering my grandfather's stories, I have to admit due embarrassment now in recalling my own Militia experiences.

My Militia memories are circa 1965/66. Little did I know then that I would return to CFB Borden in November of 1970 as an EMS Medic then for a Fundamentals of Casualty Care 6-week course. It was during the implementation of the "War Measures Act" as a result of the FLQ crisis in Quebec and heavily armed Soldiers greeted me at the Front Gate! If you'd like to take a look at one of those long-ago Howitzers we fired, check out the little-known Military Museum in

Brantford which is chock full of such old equipment. It's manned by retired servicemen and I took one of my Grandsons over there one day. While those Retired Servicemen are very knowledgeable about the featured equipment, I did impress one of them with my Gun Crew knowledge of how those Howitzers were fired.

Chapter Twenty-Nine

Dundas Entertainment

Technology-driven entertainment today never ceases to amaze me. I marveled the first time seeing my son watching a Hockey Game on his iPhone! Thinking back and remembering my earliest form of entertainment, it would be considered quasi-primitive these days. For our family it was the Radio (AM) for a long time. 900 CHML was on constantly around 16 hours a day, our window to the world and entertainment along with the Hamilton Spectator and Dundas Star Newspapers.

Paul Hanover a well known Hamilton Radio Personality was dubbed the Mayor of the Morning. I'd start every day listening to him on the radio as I sat at the Kitchen Table with my Cereal. For Kids he'd change his voice from time to time and be his sidekick "Jolly Cholly". At Night the Radio continued with the Shadow's creepy laugh or Intersanctum's creaking door followed by the scream which was the signal for my Mother to pack me off to bed. CHML featured Radio Personalities Perc Allen and Norm Marshall and later of course the famous Tom Cherrington, loved or loathed by many.

As Teen's though we all switched allegiance to CKOC who played the Top 40 for our Music that continued for many years. CHML was for old fogies! In the 1960's at CKOC, I remember Mike Jaycock joined by a young guy down from the tiny Kitchener Radio Station named Roger Ashby who would later go on to Fame in Toronto with CHUM and who could ever forget Dave Mickie or Jungle Jay Nelson.

One day when I was around 7 or so, Mary McMaster knocked at the front door and asked my Mother if she would allow me to play with her Son Graeme. McMasters lived a block up Sydenham Street at Victoria. You might recognize that House from the West Wing Television Series that was filmed there in recent years a number of times. The McMasters of course owned McMaster Pottery and were wealthy at least compared to our family.

Dundas Museum and Archives

It was at the McMaster Home that I had my first exposure to a Television which was fantastic to me! I also remember Graeme had an Aunt in Pennsylvania and when she visited she'd bring lots of Hershey's Chocolate, not available here then.

One Saturday morning up at Graeme's house I was introduced to this magic box with a small oval screen. Though it was black and white, I was absolutely fascinated as we watched Mighty Mouse, Heckle and Jeckle, Sky King and others. It was absolute magic!! I also loved Captain Kangaroo one of my early favourites. If you watched TV as a Kid in that era, who could forget the "I want my Maypo" cereal ads?

My Friend Norman's Family later on also had a small black and white TV as well. I remember watching Bing Crosby there in the Bells of St. Mary's and Going My Way at Christmas time. Norman's older Brother-in-Law worked for the newly established Dundas Cable and made his Father a remote hard-wired to the TV allowing him to mute the TV Commercials while watching his beloved New York Yankees Baseball Games. Likely the 1st TV Remote in Dundas even with its long wire control. I had barely gotten used to TV's let alone a remote!

Finally I was around 12 years old when we got our first T.V. from my Sister. She had bought a Colour TV and gave her 19-inch Black and White to us. It was just the Rabbit Ears Antennae and a bit fuzzy for the first few years until Dundas Cable arrived but it was better than the radio! Finally I got to watch the Ed Sullivan Show and could then be part of the conversation about it on Monday Mornings at School. Who could forget, Topo Gigio? Later on February 9, 1964 we tuned in along with over 70 million other people to catch the Beatles leading the British Musical Invasion. You can still enjoy Episodes of Ed Sullivan Today on YouTube.

Though Dundas was a small Town there was always entertainment happening. While "The Walking Dead" with its Zombies has become popular today, 73 years ago, a Dr. Zomb once made an appearance in Dundas! It was during my Father's tenure as a Dundas Police Officer in August of 1950. One night at the Majestic (Roxy) Theatre there was a live show featuring The Mystic Powers of Dr. Zomb. Billed as a Master Hypnotist, Dr. Zomb put an 18-year-old Girl to sleep in a bed in the Front Window of Booths Furniture Store on King Street. It was all part of an advertisement for the store. Dr. Zomb had planned to return to the Store to wake the Girl in time for the midnight show at the Theatre.

Dundas Museum and Archives

After laying there sleeping for 3 hours, the Girl got up and left the store. Later, my Father on patrol found her walking on the outskirts of Dundas. He took her back to Booths where the Show concluded. My Father was quoted at the time saying, "She didn't seem to me to be in a trance but who am I to argue with Dr. Zomb"!

At the end of May on Victoria Day, the Driving Park would be packed for the annual Fireworks Show and for kids it was an awesome evening out when we could be out well after the street lights came on! For 96 summers, the annual House of Providence Picnic was held every July 1st on the grassy slope off the Southwest Corner of Governor's Road and Ogilvie Streets. It was like a large Fun Fair with lots of games etc. One year I worked the Bingo Games there verifying winning cards while John Troy, my Grade 8 Teacher called the numbers.

The Original House of Providence, Dundas

Photo Dundas Museum and Archives

The stately structure at the top of the Hill was originally a Mansion that was known as Coleman's Castle named after its wealthy Owner, Business Man James Coleman. The Mansion was purchased by Father J. McNulty in 1879 and the first picnic was held that year to finance the balance of the purchase price of $10,000. Father McNulty turned the building over to the Sisters of St. Joseph's and the House of Providence was created as a Home for the Elderly, Orphans and Dundas area residents requiring long-term care. After a Fire severely damaged the original Mansion House, it was rebuilt in 1902. Sadly Fire would once again destroy it in 1971 and from those ashes rose the St. Joseph's Villa we all know today. The original House of Providence Picnics ended in 1975. Though it has been revived for St. Joseph's Villa it's successor this year.

In 1951, Ben and Marika Veldhuis arrived in Dundas from the Netherlands and purchased a few Greenhouses and land by the old Desjardins Canal. They created a Business which would become internationally famous for growing Cacti and Tropical Plants. The Town of Dundas sharing in such fame received permission to name a new festival, "Cactus Fest" which continues today. Later in recent years, the "Busker Fest" was also added.

Growing up as a small boy I recall other memorable community events in earlier years. There was an occasional Carnival located in the Driving Park or the downtown Memorial Square too.

Photo Dundas Museum and Archives

For many years, the large annual event was the Dundas Trade Fair. It was held at the Arena and though I wouldn't call it a Midway by any means, there were always a few rides outside the Arena. Inside it was much like a Home Show. It was a big deal though and I was always given a few dollars to go over there with and I recall taking rides on the Ferris wheel and Tilt-a-Whirl.

The Dundas Arena held many different events over the years, like the Shrine Brother's Circus. I remember watching Elephants walk through the Creek Side Large Doors and it grossed me out when they dropped their manure like loads! Though I never attended any of the Shows, there were many Musical Performers who played the Dundas Arena over the years like Louis Armstrong, Bill Haley and the Comets, Hank Williams, Hank Snow, Frankie Valli and the Four Seasons and Dionne Warwick to name a few.

Years later I recall hearing about the Dundas District High School Social Club investigating booking the Beach Boys for their Prom. As it was thousands of dollars beyond their budget it never happened of course but a bit later, the Beach Boys actually came in from Troy New York on July 21, 1969 to play the nearby Wentworth Curling Club. There was an issue with their instruments which did not arrive on time but eventually it was sorted out. That Concert I went to, sitting close to the front.

Hamilton Spectator Photo, Beach Boys with Hamilton Mayor Vic Copps

The following year, another big-time act of that era, Sly and the Family Stone were booked to play in this area. This time, once again at the Wentworth Curling Club on August 2nd, 1970 but it was a disaster! The place was packed and being a hot August Night with no air conditioning, it was like an oven inside. The Band had played only 3 songs when Sly announced, "It's too expletive hot in here" and left the stage. Fortunately, most people got their admission refunded.

Down the end of the 102 (Cootes Dr) at McMaster University were shows by the Association, Ian Thomas's Band, Tranquility Base, the Turtles, Gordon Lightfoot and many others. Lastly one could not write about Music in Dundas without mentioning the Legendary Stan Rogers in later years whose fame is right up there with Gordon Lightfoot! His tragic demise puts him in the legendary company of Patsy Cline, John Denver, Richie Valens and others. I have always enjoyed his truly Canadian Music and something I share with him is that he was born in Hamilton like me in November of 1949 on the 29th, 4 days after me!

Lastly, my Uncle was a great Wrestling Fan and took me to the Dundas Arena as a young boy many times to see the action. I remember watching Little People Wrestle and also Dick the Bulldog Brower break a chair over another wrestler's head one night. This was excitement bordering fear to watch long before learning of the theatrical aspects of such entertainment.

Chapter Thirty

Winter Fun

In long ago Dundas there was always lots of snow in the Winter and there was never a shortage of Snowmen standing guard on Neighborhood Lawns. Such creations of course were a pretty basic design from the Frosty Song though frankly a bit boring after a while.

Wouldn't you think that you could build one on your own lawn as a winter statement of sorts without any interference? Well, I thought so but one of my critics, an older lady neighbor had always been a thorn in my side, complaining to my Mother about my nearby activities. One day she called the Police saying I had a Gun out front of the House which was only a piece of pipe I happened to be playing with.

So there I was building a Snowman after a deep snowfall and as I was putting it together it started to resemble something else. As I looked it over, I thought a mushroom at first but no not quite. Sculpting away at it, a clearer picture was developing in my mind, far more interesting than a Snowman. What was growing in front of my eyes was an excited Male Anatomical Organ.

Okay well I was trying to provide a polite description but fine since you are imagining it, yes it was starting to resemble an erect frozen penis!

Finally, there it was, even with the rounder parts at the bottom! As I stood back to admire it there was still something missing and it suddenly came to me. Carefully I added a smiling face. So there it sat at the edge of the lawn, just over about 3 feet high and facing my nosey Neighbor's House of course!

Now as it was a prime Saturday Morning, I left my Lawn creation and went elsewhere to play. When I returned home later, my artful creation had been destroyed now only a jumbled pile of snow. I went inside the House to suddenly be confronted with the 3rd degree of my Mother's fury about receiving a telephone call about an obscene creation on her lawn!

Frankly I didn't feel that an artful creation closely resembling a part of male anatomy was obscene though perhaps for someone who probably hadn't seen a real one for 37 years anyway!! My excuse, learning about Penises in Health Class (white lie) failed to support my defense and as usual I was grounded for the balance of the weekend.

Snowballs were another popular pastime and while we threw them endlessly at each other and the Girls of course. There were other exciting targets too! We learned the hard way about throwing them at the School Bus where we got the Strap from Sister Marcella, the Principal at St. Augustine's. Now Cars of course were another obvious target but a careful plan for a rapid escape was required too!

The first time I remember we built a Snow Fort of sorts in front of Normans House. Being on Sydenham Street this offered a continuous stream of vehicles driving by for targets. We would load up making several snowballs in advance and wait for the unsuspecting Motorist. As the Car passed directly in front of us we'd manage a couple of volleys and then immediately drop behind our Snow Fort Wall out of sight. Most of the time, we would see the Car swerve a bit as the unsuspecting Motorist was startled but they continued on.

Occasionally if they came to a stop, the significant snow on the ground, blended the Fort Wall in perfectly and they couldn't see us. We were enjoying the fun when finally a Car Stopped but the Driver came over to the House instantly spotting our camouflaged hiding spot. It didn't go well when he knocked at Norman's front door while holding on to us firmly! Norman was ordered in the House and I was sent home, though on that occasion fortunately without a telephone call to my Mother.

We had to find a better location and shortly thereafter did we ever!

The one time Bertram House still there today of course, sits on the top of Cross Street Hill and has a nice long stone wall bordering the front of the property. It was a great hiding spot and we made snowballs waiting for the unsuspecting motorists. As the Cars came along we'd pop up like Gophers, firing quickly then drop down flattening ourselves against the wall.

Then a Dark coloured Volkswagen happened along which we should have let pass! Popping up we hammered it good with heavier packing snowballs and though it carried on, it suddenly turned around quickly and roared back up the hill. Across the back of the Bertram House we fled with an Irate Man hopping over the wall in pursuit! Around the back of the House onto Melville Street, then down the hill to Park Street where we finally lost him a block or so later. This chase featured a rather colourful soundtrack to boot with him cursing and promising what he'd do to us along the way!!

I never played organized Hockey at the Dundas Arena and suspect that the cost was prohibitive for my Mom. I certainly did skate and played Shiny Hockey on the outdoor rink at the Dundas Park. There was an upper section of the Park Snack Bar where we'd go to change out of shoes to skates. Time out there and the temperature were never a consideration for me. To this day I still have evidence of frostbite on the tops of my ears. One time it was so cold my fingers were too numb to untie my skates so I walked home in them with my shoes over my shoulders. My Mother was not impressed!

Another popular winter activity was what we called bumper sliding. When the streets were slippery we would stay low near a stop sign and once a Car stopped we would quickly sneak over to the back of it and grab hold of the back bumper. In a squatting position in your rubber boots once the car pulled away you could slide along quite a distance!

The downside as I recall, was having to inhale the exhaust fumes and of course you had to let go before the Car came to a stop or risk sliding under it. As I think back now, it does sound a bit dangerous but it was a practice that was quite popular for many kids back in the day!

Now for you old-time St. Augustine's Alumni, who could forget the infamous "Jam Piles"? The Playground slants lower even today towards Alma Street and when it snowed we would quickly make a slippery slide down towards the Street. Kids would line up and slide down, falling of course at the bottom and in quick succession a pile of young bodies would result. It was great fun though usually some unfortunate kids would suffer nose bleeds, poked eyes or goose eggs that resulted in the practice being banned! It always seemed that the really fun things were not allowed!

I'll bet most of you have long forgotten the frantic like winter wail, "Mah hung eh huck". No, not the call of an exotic Bird but a strange sound indeed. It is doubtful that many of us would be conversant with Inuktitut which is the language of our Inuit First Nations people in the far North. I certainly am not but if you place your index and second finger on your tongue and then try to say, "my tongue is stuck" it sure comes out sounding like Inuktitut.

Every Winter, we managed to trick some poor unsuspecting Kid into trying to lick the frozen Flag Pole in the St. Augustine's Play Ground. It usually started with a surprised exclamation which increased to that frantic wail throughout the Schoolyard until a Teacher came running then shortly thereafter resolving the crisis with a cup of warm water. Thereafter of course we proclaimed our innocence advising our Teacher that we had told the hapless victim not to attempt it.

Chapter Thirty-One

The Telephone

A few weeks ago, a nearby person's Cellular Telephone started to ring. It was the classic old telephone ring from long ago and brought back some memories. I wonder how many people reading this will remember what their original telephone number was back in the Day. Dundas of course had the Mayfair Exchange still maintained today though now referenced with the number 62 instead of the long-ago MA. In this age, old landline phone numbers are slowly working their way to extinction at Private Residences and even many Businesses. I even carry my own iPhone now but I still struggle to remember to take it with me everywhere.

Back in the early 50's before Dial Telephones were introduced in Dundas, my Sister Carole worked with Marie Watkins and were two of the original Bell Switch Board Operators down on Park Street. At that time you rang the Operator and asked to be connected to whomever you were calling.

Old Telephone Switchboard Dundas Museum and Archives

The Duffin telephone number was the easiest in town to remember at MA 777-7777. At 1st it was a shared "Party Line" with another number of residences. Party Lines were cheaper than Private Lines. You identified your incoming telephone calls by a distinctive ring. It was an interesting method of communication sharing a telephone line. You would pick up the phone to make a call and land right in the middle of a conversation and you would have to quickly hang up. Well, that was what you were supposed to do.

Shared lines for someone who liked to talk on the phone all day were a problem. I cannot remember if we knew who we were sharing the line with but sometimes there were issues. I recall my Mother being perturbed trying to make a phone call and some woman was still on the phone after an hour! I vaguely recall some rather terse dialogue occasionally between my Mother and whomever we shared the line with

Then there was this sneaky kid who carefully lifted the receiver to eavesdrop occasionally. "Is there someone else on this line?" Eventually Party Lines were discontinued and the line with all of the Seven's was solely ours. Yes it was ridiculously easy to remember but it also came with numerous prank calls! My Mother hung my Father's old Police Whistle on the metal phone stand near the door in the living Room. Pranksters making calls were greeted with a shrill blast of it! Dundas's Cliff's Taxi offered my Mother money to give up the line on more than one occasion but for some reason she never did.

Back in the day, as I am sure here that many will recall, a number of Street Signs were made so that they could be moved if necessary. They were often welded into large truck tire rims with the circular metal signs about 4 feet high or so. Some I recall were a temporary Bus Stop or No Parking Signs. A Truck Tire Rim was heavy enough to not be blown over by the wind but could be moved when necessary.

My apologies to my friends at the Museum but it was a long, long time ago and there are no such moveable signs there now anyway. There were though two No Parking Signs in front of the Museum and one night with our creative imaginations we struggled but managed to move one across the street to the other sidewalk. Now, we strung a clothesline wire between the 2 Signs with lots of slack, tying it off in knots to both signs.

Hiding over beside the building we waited and finally a car came along and as it hit the wire both signs were dragged into the street with a loud clanging noise.

As intended, it got a lot of attention as the Driver slammed on his brakes and a few House Doors opened as well wondering what was going on. We of course didn't wait around taking off running and laughing of course at our success. To think of it now, I know it could have been very dangerous and damaging and if a Motorcycle had come along, worse! Being two young Pranksters at the time we never considered that but at least we only did it once!

I have talked here about our Melville Street Homestead often and our downstairs apartment accessed off Sydenham Road. Of our Tenants over the years, most were very nice people. My Mother was always very respectful of our Tenants and treated them well which they very much appreciated.

Most of the time it was families with children who I sometimes played with. However, one time there was this rather strange older couple who moved in. Their names I remember well but as they have no bearing on this recollection I will leave it there. I do not recall my Mother ever having any complaints from or about a tenant of many over the years. The Husband was Mr. Magoo like with poor eyesight and the Wife was a rather rotund woman resembling a female version of Friar Tuck with fine hair and a fringed hairline.

She had a rather strange hobby to boot! Long ago, certainly before my time when a person was laid out in a Funeral Home, each Casket had a Name Plate on it. You have to wonder as in, did those paying respects not recognize the deceased? In delving into the history of this practice, it was introduced in the 17th Century primarily at the time as a sign of a once wealthy individual and eventually became widespread in the 19th Century. Furthermore, even today, most cemeteries do require that the name of the deceased be marked in the grave. I recall seeing the lid of the concrete vault my Mother's Casket was placed in. As all are now, it was painted gold and my Mothers full name had been chiseled on the lid.

As for our Downstairs Tenant, she had a collection of these Casket Name Plates with lots of different names on them proudly displayed. Okay, I did collect License Plates at one time but it was a lot less personal! So coming home from school one Monday afternoon , I got read the Riot Act from my Mother about making all this noise over the weekend! I had no idea what she was talking about as I hadn't done anything any different than normal. As well, my Mother had only been out briefly getting groceries. To make it worse, I got grounded for the following weekend.

Revenge is sweet and a few weekends later, I got together with another Friend of mine, David Penney and asked him to bring his Basketball explaining what had happened. David was only too happy to join me in Basketball dribbling practice which we did for a half an hour or so up and down the Hallway. The Phone rang and rang but we were too busy to answer it. A couple of months later our Tenants finally moved out and I don't recall my Mother being unhappy about it either.

Chapter Thirty-Two

Halloween Haunts

Around Halloween is the usual time for the recollection of Ghostly Stories, watching scary movies and the recently popular Ghost Walks in the older areas of Dundas. As Kids we often identified older Homes as Haunted Houses. For my Friends and I one of those was a House on Victoria Street, near Cross which in later years sat vacant for a long time. Though the Owners at a later time wanted to demolish it, it's heritage status saved it and it was later restored.

Our Family Homestead built in the late 1840's was far from scary though I did have an experience there one night. As a small boy given our crowded home, I slept with my Mother until about age 10 or so. Her bedroom was off the living room of the main floor. In that room there was a large bay window which looked out over the backyard. One night I was put in bed and lay there listening to her talking with someone on the telephone which was in the living room.

As I lay there, I was sure I saw the outline of a Woman standing in the window that absolutely terrified me! I dare not cause a commotion while my Mother was on the Phone so I lay there petrified watching this apparition. Once she finished the call, I let out a scream and she rushed into the bedroom and the apparition disappeared of course. It may well have been simply a reflection of light combined with my imagination but I was wide awake and not dreaming.

Now, I cannot say that I was ever an avid believer in the Supernatural but I certainly never discounted it either. For us Kids, there was another large old House at the east end of Melville Street we considered haunted across the Street and a few doors down from the Knox Presbyterian Church. It's front yard was a combination of trees and overgrown bushes like an overgrown Maze with S-shaped sidewalks. For us it was a scary place inhabited by the "Wilson

Sisters" who were two elderly ladies. From the Park Street side it sat up on the hill looking like a Gothic Mansion.

To us neighborhood kids it was a gloomy old spooky house that we were sure was haunted though likely harmless but such urban legends remain the topic of the day when the lights go out. That House is no longer there as at some point it was torn down and replaced with a Senior's like residence.

If you visit Yard Sales like we do as a hobby, Jack-O'-Lanterns are often present. Recently I came across one staring at me from a table. Immediately my mind flashed back to those Dundas Halloween Memories.

Close your eyes and remember your youth, breathing in the cool crisp fall air and that other now long-forgotten smell of Burning Leaves near the curb. Once the Leaves started to fall there was always a bonfire of sorts burning somewhere in the neighborhood. One fun practice too was to run and jump into the large raked pile of leaves before they were burned though not appreciated by the Home Owner!

My memories of Dundas back in the day on Halloween are akin to Charlie Brown's "The Great Pumpkin". Throngs of excited kids in groups wandering the streets and real carved pumpkins, candle lit with their waxy odor and scary faces staring out the window or decorating porches. No plastic pumpkins then to collect your goodies in and for my friend Norman and I, pillowcases were our containers of choice.

Living in what they now call the "Heritage District" of Dundas there were a number of large big fancier houses like the old Bertram's place and Grafton's of course at the top of the Cross Street Hill. We would always head to those types of houses first because as the Beaver would say, "they gave out good junk". So good in fact that If we were really impressed we'd go home and find something else to wear and go back for seconds!!.

I can remember my Mother questioning me on why I was changing and lying of course about being tired of wearing that first outfit. But a full-sized Chocolate Bar or even sometimes money would guarantee a return trip!

A Quarter went a long way in those days and those pillowcases would get heavy with our load of loot! Who remembers the odd house where they made you do a trick or sing or whatever before they gave you something? We were not impressed with those people and often revisited them later with soap! No one I knew ever had to have their stash checked to make sure it was safe either which is unfortunately not the case in this era in certain municipalities.

I will admit to doing that for my own kids in the 80's though not concerned so much about tampering as I was for snacking. I always managed to sneak a few of my favorites from their baskets under the guise of making sure they tasted good first! That Father Duffin, yours truly and Family lived in a very friendly neighborhood and one night I came back a bit tipsy with my son which didn't go over well with his Mother. Hey, he got his candy and I just happened to be plied with a few liquid treats here and there. A poor man supporting his child in that cool air did not refuse a comforting glass of spirits! But, I digress so let's carry on about an old Dundas Halloween.

To this day, I continue to love Halloween and always make sure we have "Good Junk" on hand to hand out. Times have changed though with fewer kids, some safety issues and of course that frightening and tiring pandemic that in full force a few years ago now really put a dent in Halloween Fun. With most restrictions now lifted hopefully future years will be more fun for the Kids.

I am not sure there is such a thing anymore like "Devils Night," but back then it was always on the night before Halloween and really was way too much of an adventure to miss being at home. Though at our age we couldn't be out too late, the end of Daylight Savings time and the early darkness that followed was a perfect setting especially if it landed on a Friday or Saturday Evening.

My Friend Norman had a subscription to "Boys Life" Magazine. It was a relatively large magazine like the old "Life" ones. There were quite a few stacked up in his basement. For whatever reason, most of the time we were left unattended down there, which we really appreciated. If we had been over at my house, well you know about my Mother, we'd have been under a magnifying glass especially on that particular evening.

Back then, chock full of imagination we always managed to come up with some interesting ideas. One popular Devil's Night Prank as many of you will remember was to take a bar of soap and rub it on the windows of cars parked along the streets and the odd House. While it was a fun prank of sorts for the Soaper, it soon became boring and you never got to see the Soapee's reaction once it was discovered. On this night though we decided to make a life like Dummy. I have no recollection of why, it just seemed like a good idea at the time.

So there we were stuffing rolled-up magazines into the arms and legs of an old shirt and pants. In the absence of any religious considerations we nailed it to a cross we fashioned from a bunch of 2 X 4's. A rubbery mask version of an old man's head and face looked good once stuffed with old newspapers and tacked on. We also found a coil of old rope which we took with us as well. The challenge then came of sneaking our creation out of the House past his Parents and Sister. This involved lugging it up the stairs thru their Kitchen and out the back door once the coast was clear.

The Cross was not light by any means as we trudged along with it and the smaller Lawn Mower Gasoline can, up Cross Street towards the Park. It is remarkable now to recall this and wonder how two kids carrying a Dummy on a Cross with a gas can and rope were not stopped or questioned by anyone! As we entered the Park Gates though, a ring of flashlights appeared and we were quickly shooed away. They were obviously prepared for the evening's Hi Jinx. Okay, travel with us, now up Alma Street past St. Augustine's School across Sydenham with our life-sized Crucifix which was really starting to get heavy.

We then headed up Queen Street to the end and lashed it to a metal street sign. I remember us standing there taking turns splashing gas on it and us and trying to get it going by lighting it with matches. After a few tries it still wouldn't light, then suddenly with a loud WHOMP up in flames it went and literally set us back on our butts!

A Front Door opened a few Houses down the street and a woman screamed. I guess from a distance away it might have looked like a real person burning. It was truly a miracle that we somehow didn't set ourselves on fire. Now that famous Fog Horn wail erupted in the distance from the Central Fire Hall and we took off down the nearby creek bed. I slipped and fell breaking the eggs I was carrying in my pocket that I had intended to throw around later. Later arriving home, smelling of gasoline and a coat pocket full of egg yuck,

I did face an extreme interrogation but managed to pawn it off on practicing for an upcoming school project. Of course my Mother didn't believe me but I did manage to escape severe discipline. Though we had once again managed to get away with it without being caught in retrospect we were very lucky. Norman's name and address were printed on the cover of those magazines which either burned off or weren't noticed. No CSI in those days!

Chapter Thirty-Three

A Real Ghost

Continuing with the Halloween theme, just up the hill from Dundas though in Ancaster, I once had an incredible experience. I believe given what I was told later that I had an encounter with a real Ghost. The former Dundas Teen Town Wallflower having become a Disc Jockey, had this successful Business on the side for over 20 years. Having a full-time EMS Career, I did have the opportunity to play music at a number of area Emergency Services Dances.

Twice in the early 80's, I played the music for the Christmas Dances for the former Ancaster Fire Department. These Parties took place in the Old Ancaster Town Hall up on Wilson Street. That Building was actually constructed in 1868. While some well-known spectral locations in Ancaster would be the Hermitage and the Coach and Lantern Pub, my experience was in the Old Town Hall there and I will never forget it. If you have ever had the opportunity to visit this historic building, you would remember it is a hall with a relatively small interior space with a stage at one end, no more than about 15 feet wide.

So it was during the Christmas Holidays and the Hall was filled with around a 100 or so people. Having read a number of stories of hauntings, one consistent aspect is the energy in the air that apparently energizes the Spirits. So imagine being in a location, well over a hundred years old and full of people with loud music reverberating off the walls. At that time I used dual Turntables playing 45 rpm records. It was a successful Party and as I spun the tunes of the day, I used to shuffle those records not unlike playing cards finding songs based on the colour of the record labels.

The Windows had been decorated as shown in the photo to resemble how it had looked in long ago Christmas's with large Wreaths in the tall narrow Church like Windows with candles, electric now in the center of them. As well the Hall was festooned with bright red bows in concert with a "Dickens Era" appearance. There was only one way to the Stage from behind me and I was set up only a few feet from the edge of it. To my right in the corner there was a decorated Christmas tree.

As I shuffled thru the records at some point in the later evening, I glanced up and noticed a Man standing on the stage with me over by the Christmas tree. We briefly locked eyes as he stared intently at me, his face expressionless and his appearance was quite solid. It was his vintage clothing that caught my attention with his formal long coat with a velvet-like vest.

His Shirt was bright white and high-collared with a narrow red ribbon-like tie around his neck and his hair was quite short and dark.

While it was a momentary glance, my initial thought at the time was this person was costumed for the occasion as he fits perfectly with the Victorian-like decorations. A few moments later, I looked up again and he was gone. Being busy, I never gave it much thought and went on with my business wondering how he had managed to get on the stage without walking past me. It was the only way someone could have gotten over there as that side of the stage was stacked with tables and chairs.

Around 11 p.m. the music was briefly stopped to allow for some Door Prizes to be drawn and I had to pause while someone went out to their Car to bring in another prize. While waiting I remarked about how authentic the Vintage Decorations were congratulating those who had arranged them. I then also mentioned the gentleman who was attired in the period clothing asking him wherever he was to stand up for all of the Guests to see. Everyone looked around and there was a murmur in the crowd but no one stood up. I never gave it another thought and finished the night.

Later while I was packing up I was approached by a Lady who advised that she was a member of the Ancaster Historical Society. She went on to say that I had seen the Ghost of one of the Town Councilors of that era whose name escapes me now. Apparently he had been seen before during other events there. The Man I saw certainly for me did not resemble the classic Ghost description as he was quite solid in his appearance and standing only 10 or 15 feet from me. The following Christmas I was back there again playing music for their Party and all night long my eyes were riveted to every nook and cranny though I never saw a thing!

So there it is, my Ghost encounter though I never realized it as it happened, but I will say I certainly did not imagine it and know what I saw. Given the history of this area, I am sure there are many other untold experiences of the supernatural to be shared on a Halloween Evening. Many Folks might be surprised to know that the Village of Ancaster is the 3rd oldest community in Ontario behind Kingston and Niagara on the Lake. It was once so politically significant that it was under serious consideration to become Upper Canada's Capital City before Ottawa was ultimately selected.

Before we leave this chapter, we couldn't do so without mentioning a few other notable supernatural Dundas Tales.

Completed in 1929, the historic Gothic Collegiate-designed Dundas District School, sits just at the bottom of the escarpment on King Street in Dundas. When it first opened its doors it was a high school, then became a middle school, and has since been converted into condominiums after closing its doors for good in 2007. The ghost tales at Dundas District vary and there are many. But the two most prevalent accounts always center on a janitor named Russell and a temporary morgue.

As the legend goes, the haunting of Russell all started with a pact between five custodians. The agreement? Whoever passed away first was to come back and haunt their Co-Workers and the school. As fate would have it, Russell, the practical joker of the bunch, was the first to pass on. How fitting. There have been what seems to be dozens of eyewitness accounts of Russell, many by the caretakers who partook in the pact, as well as former students. Some of the sightings include hallways being mopped while a janitor was on break, lockers rattling at the end of hallways, jingling of keys, the squeaky wheels of his mop bucket, and a whistling melody echoing through the cold, eerie, corridors. Apparently the place Russell was spotted most was inside the shadowy, unnerving auditorium.

But that's not the only spectral occurrence that District High School was noted for.. The other story is darker and more chilling. On Christmas Day of 1934, over 20 years earlier than the aforementioned janitor pact, two Trains collided on the railroad tracks just above the school. 18 people died in the crash and given it's close-by location, the school was used as a temporary morgue.

The Hamilton Spectator

Thereafter, Ghostly occurrences were often recorded of Laughter, cries for help, and mischief allegedly played out by those spirits. A former caretaker recalled seeing five shadows while cleaning and when he went to move his mop, he couldn't. One of the ghosts was holding it down, leaving him frozen and helpless until they vanished.

Another notable story involved former principal Peter Greenberg. Motion detector alarms went off late in the night and the police notified him in the morning about the incident. They said nothing had happened, but when the principal got to his office he heard "banging and clanging" upstairs. After calling the police, they went in to investigate. It was on the third floor, and they could hear kids, glasses breaking, and heavy footsteps in a classroom down the hall. When they opened the door not a thing was out of place and the noises stopped completely. Greenberg said he never believed any of the stories were true until that day.

The stories and urban legends of Dundas District have continued over the years. Many residents of this quaint, picturesque town have heard the stories. They've seen Russell, and if they haven't, their parents have or their friends have. One thing is for certain, even if you don't believe in ghosts, it's hard not to believe all the eyewitness accounts over the years, especially in a school that was as old as District. (Thomas Allen – Urban City)

We can only wonder if the same spirits still wander the area now. Is Russell cleaning anyone's floor? Are there mysterious noises at night or strange shadows? These legends live on and are somehow fitting in the History of the former Valley Town.

Chapter Thirty-Four

Winter Adventures

Snowballs were another popular pastime and while we threw them endlessly at each other and the Girls of course. There were other exciting targets too! We learned the hard way about throwing them at the School Bus where we got the Strap from Sister Marcella, the Principal at St. Augustine's. Now cars of course were another obvious target but a careful plan for a rapid escape was required too!

The first time, I remember we built a Snow Fort of sorts in front of Normans House. Being on Sydenham Street this offered a continuous stream of vehicles driving by for targets. We would load up making several snowballs in advance and wait for the unsuspecting Motorist. As the Car passed directly in front of us we'd manage a couple of volleys then immediately drop behind our Snow Fort Wall out of sight. Most of the time, we would see the Car swerve a bit as the unsuspecting Motorist was startled but they continued on.

Occasionally if they came to a stop, the significant snow on the ground, blended the Fort Wall in perfectly and they couldn't see us. We were enjoying the fun when finally a Car Stopped but the Driver came over to the House instantly spotting our camouflaged hiding spot. It didn't go well when he knocked at Norman's front door while holding on to us firmly! Norman was ordered in the House and I was sent home, though on that occasion fortunately without a telephone call to my Mother.

We had to find a better location and shortly thereafter did we ever!

The one time Bertram House still there today of course, sits on the top of Cross Street Hill and has a nice long stone wall bordering the front of the property. It was a great hiding spot and we made the snowballs waiting for the unsuspecting motorists. As the Cars came along we'd pop up like Gophers, firing quickly then drop down flattening ourselves against the wall.

Then a Dark coloured Volkswagen happened along which we should have let pass! Popping up we hammered it good with heavier packing snowballs and though it carried on, it suddenly turned around quickly and roared back up the hill. Across the back of the Bertram House we fled with an Irate Man hopping over the wall in pursuit! Around the back of the House onto to Melville Street then down the hill to Park Street where we finally lost him a block or so later. This chase featured a rather colourful soundtrack to boot with him cursing and promising what he'd do to us along the way!!

Another popular winter activity was what we called bumper sliding. When the streets were slippery we would stay low near a stop sign and once a car stopped we would quickly sneak over to the back of it and grab hold of the back bumper. In a squatting position in your rubber boots once the car pulled away you could slide along quite a distance!

The downside as I recall was having to inhale the exhaust fumes and of course you had to let go before the Car came to a stop or risk sliding under it. As I think back now, it does sound a bit dangerous but it was a practice that was quite popular for many kids back in the day!

Now for you old-time St. Augustine's Alumni, who could forget the infamous "Jam Piles". The Playground slants lower even today towards Alma Street and when it snowed we would quickly make a slippery slide down towards the Street. Kids would line up and slide down, falling of course at the bottom and in quick succession, a pile of young bodies would result. It was great fun though usually some unfortunate kids would suffer nose bleeds, poked eyes or goose eggs that resulted in the practice being banned! It always seemed that the really fun things were not allowed!

I 'll bet most of you have long forgotten the frantic like winter wail, "Mah hung eh huck". No, not the call of an exotic Bird but a strange sound indeed. It is doubtful that many of us would be conversant with Inuktitut which is the language of our Inuit First Nations people in the far North. I certainly am not but if you place your index and second finger on your tongue then try to say, "My Tongue is Stuck" it sure comes out sounding like Inuktitut.

Every winter we managed to trick some poor unsuspecting kid into trying to lick the frozen Flag Pole in the St. Augustine's Play Ground. It usually started with a surprised exclamation which increased to that frantic wail throughout the School yard until a Teacher came running then shortly thereafter resolving the crisis with a cup of warm water. Thereafter of course we proclaimed our innocence advising that we had told the hapless victim not to attempt it.

Chapter Thirty-Five

Historic Fires

Now I'll take you back to February of 1979 to 46 King Street in Dundas when the original building structure was still there housing Lillian's Dress Shop. It was severely gutted by a Fire.

Now hop on the Time Machine and let's go back another 16 years or so when this same address housed the Valley Town Restaurant with it's large Marquee like sign. There also was a significant Fire there in the winter that gutted it as well.

Photo Dundas Museum and Archives

Though I could not find any specific information on either Fire, it is nonetheless interesting given the exact same location and time of year. Given the age of the structures and types of businesses, heating, wiring and/or kitchen equipment were likely factors. As electrical fires go, there was another one just a few years ago started by the Christmas Tree Lights at the Village Bakery.

As for the Valley Town Fire I recall a few teenage boys who just happened to be hanging out a few days later behind the restaurant. A rather flimsy rear door was noted and a plan was hatched to come back after dark. While there was no "break-in" per se, the rear door was easily entered and I remember the strong smell of the burned interior. While it was dim inside, those very bright streetlights of the Sixties provided a sufficient glow for us to look around. I tripped over a great find in the dimly lit corridor. 5 or 6 pop cases of various flavours lined the Hallway. As many will remember back in the day, pop cases were wooden containing 4 cardboard, and 6 packs of glass pop bottles. This was a great find versus a few large cans of vegetables and Tomato Sauce etc.

I would have never been able to explain to my Mother how I came to find a large smoky can of vegetables. Mind you, none of us could explain suddenly bringing home cartons of burnt-smelling pop either. The time of year and weather though was very advantageous. Behind the Roxy Theatre, in between it and the Mountain View Dairy was a stretch of snow covered ground sufficiently deep enough to cover and chill the Pop which we enjoyed for several weeks.

Once again my Mother was mystified, this time on what had happened to our bottle opener? Former Dundas Police Officer Ron Peraziana would tell you that you don't have to break anything when unlawfully entering a premises to be charged with Break and Enter. Fortunately for us, the missing aspect here that was missing was not being found in the "enter" either.

Before we leave 46 King Street West, lets crank the Time Machine again and go back to the mid-Fifties. In this photo, Look at the Sign above the same location then which appears to be a large Tea Pot. Being a youngster then I am straining my memory but I am sure it was a Restaurant then too, perhaps "Moms Blue Kitchen"?

Photo Dundas Museum and Archives

My Brother being 6 years my senior was almost a generation ahead of me growing up in Dundas and his crowd were obviously different from mine. I will note a few of those names here for posterity. Frank "Busty" Fama, Walter "Tex" Rogerson, Bill McGinley, Danny, Pat and Paul Penney, (my friend their younger Brother, David), Ernie Blandin, Bill Grisdale, Jerome Duckworth, Mike Cahill, and so on. I hope that some of these folks are still with us to read this.

Note the photo here of my Brother Billy and Alex McDonald on their way to school in September of 1958. Alex lived at the House of Providence where his Father was the Maintenance Man.

Chapter Thirty-Six

The Santa Suit and Other Christmas Stories

My Siblings and I were raised Roman Catholic after my Mother had originally converted and became Catholic for my Father. I am not sure about how strict our Church Attendance was before he passed away but I imagine given he was a 3rd Degree Knight of Columbus, that our Family was always there on Sundays. My Brother Billy was the Top Altar Boy for a Number of Christmas Eve Services. As I grew older though I remember it was only at Christmas and Easter that Church Attendance was strictly enforced so there we'd be at St. Augustine's on Christmas morning.

Now in the Duffin Homestead on Melville Street, the Door to the Living Room where the Christmas Tree was located, was closed and out of bounds until after Church. Yep, nothing like knowing about all those presents just sitting there begging to be opened and not even being allowed to have a look! Well at least while anyone else was looking. I'd wait for my Mother to have her bath and once I was sure she was in the tub I would stealthily creep into the Living Room through her Bedroom Door.

This left the Main Door off the front Hallway closed, while the rest of the family was either upstairs or in the Kitchen. Quietly crawling on my hands and knees with some Scotch Tape, I would arrive at the presents piled high looking for my name. As I came across them, I'd make a slight tear in the paper at the bottom, enough to figure out what it was then tape it back up. Later, I sat in Church drooling at the thought of going back home to open them. I think I said a silent prayer to God not to worry and I would check back in with him later. Coming back and ripping under the Tree, I gave my best Academy Award Performance with surprise and glee with my presents.

There was a stand of Pine Trees up the hill from what we called McKenzie's Cave and one Christmas, my Brother chopped one down perhaps 15 feet or so high and cut off the top 6-7 feet dragging it down the Mountain to the House. I remember my Mother pouring 7 UP Pop into the container. I just found it in the woods he said.

My Brother and his Friend Wayne Sorci once told their St. Augustine's Grade 8 Teacher that his Friend owned a Christmas Tree Farm and they could get a free Tree for the School. They got the afternoon off school and snuck onto the Dundas Golf Course cutting a Tree down there to bring back to school.

Young Allan with the Robinson's Department Store Santa circa 1955

To make money for the Christmas Gifts that I'd buy at the Pinder's Store, my Friend Norman and I would shovel snow off sidewalks. We'd walk up Melville Street to the end then come back along Park Street. It always seemed to snow more back then, especially right before Christmas and on a good day, 10 Bucks for our efforts was not out of the question, a fortune to us!

Many years later, now with a Son and Daughter of my own, I used to arrange the Christmas Parties at the Ambulance Service my partner Dennis Munch and I operated in Oakville. I would go to the National Film Board's office in the Federal Building at Main and Caroline in Hamilton and rent some 16 mm Cartoon Reels. We would take a sheet out of an Ambulance and hang it on our large Garage Wall taping the Garage Door Windows with black plastic garbage bags.

We would then line up some chairs that created our Theatre and we entertained the kids while a cauldron of wieners was boiled for Hot Dogs. Our connections with Oakville Dairy provided chocolate milk and small ice cream sundaes to finish off the Christmas Party refreshments. Santa would arrive after lunch making a grand entrance in an Ambulance, Siren Blaring to pass out the gifts to the kids. We always checked in advance to find out how many kids were in the pediatric ward of the Oakville Hospital where we'd take Santa with a bag of gifts later.

The Santa Suit shown in the first photo here with my Son Brad was cheap and very well-worn corduroy with a scruffy Beard and Hair. Though I never played Santa at the Children's parties I did inherit the Suit and did manage to pull it off successfully at Home with my Kids. One year after Christmas I put the Suit and accompaniments in a plastic garbage bag for storage. My wife accidentally put it out with the trash! It was a very easy mistake which I totally understood and gave it no further thought at the time. She felt so bad about it though that she went out and paid a fortune for a new Velvet Santa suit, including the belt, boot covers and an expensive beard and wig.

You can appreciate the significant difference in the 2nd photo of a much more realistic Santa where I am holding my inquisitive daughter Kelly beside her Grandfather, Howard Whatmough.

The kids never noticed and I continued for a couple of years, until the question arose of why I never happened to be there when Santa came. From then on it was a neighbor or other relative playing Santa continuing the magic and for our subsequent generations, that Suit is still being worn today!

My Sister Carole was the Cosmetician at the Amherst Drug Store in Dundas for a couple of years in the mid 80's working for the very popular and respected Druggist Hilton Silberg. Many of you will remember this store which was originally located beside the grocery store at Ogilvie and Governors Road. Carole lived just up the street at the Governor's Green Building.

Knowing my Sister, she was no doubt bragging about how wonderful a Santa Claus I was to Hilton one day. Hilton decided that he would love to have Santa arriving at the drugstore, one Saturday morning as a promotion. When they asked me, I said absolutely not. My Sister kept at me and finally I agreed to a two-hour command performance in exchange for a 40-ounce bottle of rum!

So there I was, having been snuck in a back door well ahead to dress. As I came out and walked down an aisle, I was initially relieved as I didn't see any kids and thought it wasn't going to be that bad after all. Then I turned the corner and froze as the numerous children lined up in and even outside the store started screaming in unison! Okay, well I was a Parent of course but having numerous snotty-nosed kids climbing on to me was a definite once in a lifetime experience! My imagination soared as I explained what my Elves were busy building and how I was going to have to round up Rudolph and the Boys to get the Sleigh Flying. Boy those Elves were surely going to be busy though trying to find He Man and Cabbage Patch Dolls that I had already been looking for high and low for months!

Initially it seemed to be going fine and then suddenly looking up, I froze again. It was akin to a Ghost like vision of a Christmas Past. They're waiting patiently, with I presume her husband by her side, she was my dream girl from my days at Parkside High School. A girl I had never even had the nerve to speak to but had always secretly admired from a distance.

They stood there with three of the worst-behaved children I had ever seen and as they literally jumped on my lap it took a supreme effort to retain my balance and keep my beard and hair from being pulled off! What they asked for would have filled a Railway Car though I will admit I had visions of items with Bars! I did my best and survived unscathed though silently counting my blessings that I had remained a distance from her earlier in life and like Ebenezer Scrooge, imagining what might have been.

Photo Val Harvey Patterson

Chapter Thirty-Seven

Some More Memories

Given my Father's occupation as a Police Officer in Dundas, it would only be appropriate here to share a bit of that Police History. During my father's tenure with the Dundas Police in the early 50's there were only 3 Police Cruisers covering the Town during peak hours. In the evening that was reduced to 2 with each officer covering half the town. The Police Department was on a lower level of the Town Hall off Hatt Street. For the real criminals, there was one cell located there though usually utilized as a holding cell until they could be transported to Hamilton.

Earl Jack was Chief of Police at the time my Father joined the Force, then later in that era it was Sam Eyre a fellow Constable with my Father who would go on to become Chief. Some of the Dundas and area Boys who later became it's Police Officers back then were, Mike Driscoll, Bill Coomber, Bill Mushing, Bernie Evans, Dennis Carr, Al Wilson, Bill Littlewood, Ron Shaidle and of course Ron Peraziana who went to St. Augustine's with my Brother Billy. Ron joined the Dundas Police in 1966, Badge # 18. Given the small-town atmosphere, while there was certainly crime to deal with it was not of today's magnitude.

What follows is of a lighter humorous fare. This photo is of my Father, circa 1950 with Dundas Police Chief Earl Jack attempting to mount a wayward Horse.

During the infamous Dundas Ravine Bashes, given the volume of Police Officers on Duty, assistance was brought in for a number of raids from the O.P.P. While unofficially noted, during one of those raids two young men somehow escaped the Police and managed to either camouflage themselves or had passed out in the Bushes. When they came out of the Ravine the following morning they were covered in rashes having spent the night in a Poison Ivy patch!

As previously noted, Television didn't come along for me until 12 years old or so. Entertainment for our family was the Radio that played music and news all day and evening tuned to 900 CHML. One day this small boy received a gift of an old Tube Radio from the 1940's from one of my Uncles. While I don't recall the manufacturer, it was an A.M. and Shortwave Radio and had an illuminated map of the world on it's dial. My Mother helped him carry it upstairs to my room and it was a fantastic treasure.

I plugged it in and listened to the Shortwave signaling of squeals, whistles and roaring static as I turned the dial picking up bits and pieces of programming fading in and out. The first clear transmission I received was a tick, tick, tick sound followed by a disembodied voice droning, " NRC, Eastern Daylight Time, 21 hours 14 minutes and 10 seconds". Not being aware of the 24-hour clock, I found the time and voice scary and quickly turned the dial. Later, I learned that NRC meant the National Research Council of Canada. They maintain our Country's National Official Clock in Ottawa. It is broadcast as noted in hours, minutes and seconds every 10 seconds. You can find the phone number online and it is an interesting listen for a matter of a few seconds. Our Emergency Agencies used to call regularly to ensure their recorded time was accurate.

I also heard the Voice of America which is an international broadcast that provides news, information and cultural programming in over 40 different languages throughout the world. In the broadcast of radio frequencies, without becoming too technical, Emergency Services used to operate on VHF Radio Frequencies. Occasionally certain atmospheric weather conditions would cause what is known as "skip" where faraway radio transmissions can be received locally. In the early 70's in our Ambulances, occasionally we would hear Ohio State Police Communications crystal clear on our radios.

One Saturday Night as the young Dundas Boy sat in the dark, slowly turning the dial, a loud clear signal suddenly was received. It was the Kiwi Gospel Hour live from Auckland New Zealand over 13,000 Kms away. There I was sitting in the Dundas Valley and listening to it which totally amazed me.

Now fast forward over a dozen years later and I was married and no longer living in Dundas. The old radio was still in my former room of our Dundas House and I sold it to a Friend who went over to pick it up. As my Mother and he were carrying it down the stairs, out popped a secret drawer near the base of the Radio which I had long forgotten about. My friend noticing this and it's contents quickly closed it. Unbeknownst to him as they twisted and turned going down the stairs, it happened again. This time it was my Mother who noticed and quickly closed it.

A number of years previously I had been, um, visiting with a young lady up there when my Mother had unexpectedly returned home early from a Cottage weekend. In our frantic rush to get dressed, she had left her unmentionables up there. Later discovering this I quickly stashed them away in that secret spot which I had long forgotten.

The foregoing descriptions were provided by both my Friend and my Mother later telling me their versions of it. All my Mother said was, "I don't want to know" and for those enquiring minds, no, the apparel did not belong to any Dundas area Girl either!!

So anyone who knew Marty Zuliniak well would know that in his early Teenage Days he held court often so to speak at Ernie Mustard's Pool Hall. On many days after High School was out, a number of us would gather there and of course in the summer. I went to Parkside while Marty went to the District. In those days from my recollection is that the Dundas District High School was smaller than Parkside where I attended. The Student volume at Parkside was over 1100 Kids. Given that volume there had to be two shifts, mine was earliest from 8 a.m. to 2:30 while a second ran from 9 a.m. to 4.

That allowed me to complete my Spectator Route immediately after school and plenty of time to meet the Guys at Mustard's later. So we'd play Snooker Pool over and over but for me there was no gradual improvement, I was simply terrible at it. In retrospect, I am surprised they continued to allow me to play especially when we'd bet money on the game. You can google the rules of snooker, too many for a description here but when 4 people play, the person who sinks the yellow ball and the person who sinks the black ball become partners with their scores combined.

In the earlier days, Marty Zuliniak, Bruce Ralston and I played quite a number of games with various other players being the 4th. Anyone in the Hall when I was partnered with Bruce would remember. Bruce could be quite theatrical on occasion and would scream and yell in frustration when I missed an easy shot. AGGGH DUFFIN!!!!!! (expletive) Muffin Man, sometimes on the floor feinting a Heart Attack! A very, very funny Guy. We'd be warned a number of times to keep the noise down.

When recalling those old Dundas Days at Mustard's, there is another name for mandatory inclusion here. One of the most famous Players of Pool (Billiards) was Minnesota Fats. In Dundas back in the day we had our own! He certainly wasn't fat by any means or very tall for that matter either. But anyone ever gracing the door of Mustard's would remember Joe McDonald who was lethal with a pool cue in emptying a table! I have no idea if Joe ever went professional but he was absolutely one of the best!

Check out this photo taken by Marty Zuliniak at the front of the Pool Hall, circa 1969 and note the Nick Names of these individuals. Perhaps some reading this will recognize a few of them but I have chosen not to note their actual names here as once they went thru that door, they were known by their appointed nicknames. Marty with his creative imagination had a nickname for everyone. While Las Vegas had the first one, this could be considered old Dundas's "Rat Pack".

L to R, Brew Go, Pig Pen, Dewey, DJ, Pointer, Pixie, OD Bil, Beer Bottle, Wench and Rats

Like many small towns back in the day, Dundas had a number of Variety Stores popular then for Cigarettes and Candy. I have mentioned O'Neil's, but when I think of such stores there was also Wilson's farther downtown and operated by a Little person Kenny and over at Park Street and York Road was Whites. Hanging from the ceiling behind the counter there was the quite large head of an Indigenous Woman of long ago which frightened this small boy. In Greensville, while the Post Office also sold merchandise too, it was Fenton's Gocery that was popular in that area.

The Dairy Bar provided all of our Ice Cream requirements. I remember my then future Wife Judy Whatmough's Sister Joan worked there one summer scooping Ice Cream and her biceps put mine to shame!

Valley City Dairy Bar Dundas Museum and Archives

Another Ice Cream Shop for a limited time was Kuhn's Dairy Isle which featured soft ice cream and pre-frozen Ice Cream rolls you pulled the wrapper off. Kuhn's was down near the end of Hwy 102 (Coote's Drive) and that building later became the Dundas Swap Shop.

While my memory of teenage jobs focused on us Boys, the Girls as above also had employment at different activities. Judy worked for a period of time at the Sherwood Farms Chicken Processing Plant in West Flamboro. Their business featured the freshest chicken which you had to order literally the day before and may have been walking around the morning of the day it was ready for pickup in a carton with dry ice.

Sherwood Farms Chicken Processing Line

Judy's job did not involve much chicken though as her position was at the end of the line where only the feet remained and had to be thrown into a large cardboard barrel.

I recall recoiling in horror the first time I saw a tub of chicken feet while with my Mother at the Hamilton Farmer's Market. Fortunately they were never added to the list of other items I considered non-edible. Though I have never cooked them, there is an endless list of recipes for their use including Broth.

Newly Wed Joe and Betty Penney, Nova Scotia

Chapter Thirty-Eight

Some Penneys for your Thoughts

Joseph Penney seeking employment to better support his family travelled west. He arrived in Dundas in 1951 finding a job at Bertram's Manufacturing. The following summer Wife Betty, with 6 Kids and Farm Hand Henry in tow, arrived by Train in Hamilton. Henry had been a loyal Worker on the Farm. As he had no relatives there, Mrs. Penney wasn't leaving him behind. As the saying down East goes, they were and remain the "Salt of the Earth".

R.L. Betty, Pat, Paul, Danny, Nancy. F. David, Joe (Dad), Mary, Betty (Mom) and Michael

The Penney Family

I had the pleasure of playing their Dance Music twice for large Family gatherings. Once up the hill in the old Greensville Town Hall and then on another occasion at the Dundas Legion. The Penney

Family's original digs was the last House up Queen Street in Dundas just before the original Quarry there. With their incredible Family of 8 children, it was no doubt challenging for their Parents but they obviously excelled in raising "good people" and with considerable musical talent to boot.

The Penneys were a very musically inclined family and could easily have become a Family Band with their combined talents.

Paul actually performed in an early 60's Group the T Birds that he and some fellow Soldiers of the Canadian Armed Forces formed while stationed in Germany to the delight of the local frauleins.

The T Birds 1963 Paul Penney R

The Penney Family

Anyone who chummed around with Penney Kids would never forget Mrs. Penney's homemade bread. For my Brother Billy, Pat and Paul were his buddies and for me being younger it was David who I was proud to call my friend. On the fairer side of the fence were the Penney Girls, Nancy, Betty and Mary. David and I were good friends though I didn't appreciate it though when he bought Colleen Gary a ring from Pinders! But hey at least I was the first Boy to kiss her and she actually was the 1st Girl I ever kissed. At the end of the day though, neither one of us were successful in gaining her favour and she went away to a private Girl's School. David and I did though, remain great friends!

I don't ever recall being in the Penney Household without that beautiful fresh bread scent wafting through out it. Despite Mother Penney's warnings we would get into it while it was still too warm and suffer the belly aches that followed.

Then there were the Boat Projects Father Penney had worked on or assisted with over the years. From this young boy's viewpoint, the mixing of the fiberglass looked like concrete to me and I was convinced they would never float! After one was completed, before it could be moved, the Garage had to be dismantled. I have no idea how many Boats where created by Mr. Penney up on Queen Street in Dundas but have always remembered them.

I have finally reconnected with David again and discovered he lives in Halifax, Nova Scotia having returned to his family's roots with his Brother Pat. Paul and Michael remain in the Dundas area.

***

Here we are now, at the conclusion of this book. Thank you for joining me on this journey through my memories of growing up in what was then the small town of Dundas, back in a much simpler time. It is my sincere wish that if you, too, grew up in Dundas or any other small town, this book has sparked many of your own memories. It has often been said that "the best thing about memories is making them," though we never realized it at the time.

Within the confines of my mind, there runs a constant video, reanimating old Dundas and many of our friends and the characters we knew, all set against Norman Rockwell-like backgrounds. For me, it brings the Dundas of my youth back to life, along with many people and places that no longer exist. I left our town after spending my initial

20 years there. However, I have always carried it deep inside me, and each time I saw the name Dundas elsewhere, it warmed my heart.

Today, I reside just minutes away from the community where I was raised and often visit. I am fortunate to now be so close by. If you peruse Dundas's social media posts, you will find many former Dundasians now living abroad throughout the world. They, too, have retained memories of their youth in long-ago Dundas.

In my humble opinion, regardless of recent criticisms of many of our forefathers for their beliefs beyond today's standards, it was never those names or reputations that governed our lives. Dundas then and now remains a community populated by caring people who enjoy living and supporting each other in its small-town atmosphere.

Though the town of Dundas is no more, the community remains alive and well! As the local saying goes "Dundas will always be Dundas" and it's community spirit and heartbeat continue to resonate throughout the valley, as it has for over 200 years. I hope you have enjoyed these stories of my adventures as much as I have in reliving them.

Ma Penney With Her Boys

The Penney Family

Epilogue

So, here we are now at this book's conclusion. Thank you for joining me along my trail of memories growing up in what was then the Small Town of Dundas, back in a much simpler time. It is my sincere wish that if you too grew up in Dundas or any other Small Town, this book has sparked a number of your own memories. It has often been said that "the best thing about memories was making them" though we never realized it at the time.

Between my ears runs this constant video reanimating old Dundas and many of our Friends and characters we knew and their roles in Norman Rockwell like settings. For me it brings the Dundas of my youth back to life along with people and places that no longer exist. I left our Town after spending my initial 20 years there. I have always carried it deep inside me though and each time I saw the name Dundas elsewhere, it always warmed my heart.

Today, I reside mere minutes away from the community where I was raised and often visit. I am so fortunate to now be so close by. If you look thru the Dundas Social Media posts you will find many former Dundasians now expatriates throughout the world. They too have still retained those memories of their youth in long-ago Dundas.

It is my humble opinion that regardless of the recent criticism's of many of our Forefathers for their beliefs beyond today's standards, it was never those names or reputations that governed our lives. Dundas then and now remains a community populated by caring people who enjoy living and supporting each other in it's small-town atmosphere.

Though the Town of Dundas is no more, it certainly lives on! It's community spirit and heartbeat continues to resonate throughout the Valley as it has for over 200 years. I hope you have enjoyed these stories of my adventures as much as I have had in reliving them.

Manufactured by Amazon.ca
Bolton, ON